Social Construction

Entering The Dialogue

By Kenneth J. Gergen
And Mary Gergen

Taos Institute Publications
Chagrin Falls, Ohio

SOCIAL CONSTRUCTION
Entering The Dialogue

COVER ART: Designed by Anna Maria Rijsman-Lecluyse and reproduced with
permission.

SECOND PRINTING 2008

FIRST EDITION

Copyright © 2004 by Kenneth J. Gergen and Mary Gergen

Taos Institute Publications

Chagrin Falls, Ohio

ISBN-13: 978-0-7880-2127-5
ISBN 10: 0-7880-2127-3
LCN: 2004111206   PRINTED IN USA

Introduction To Taos Institute Publications

The Taos Institute is a nonprofit organization dedicated to the development of social constructionist theory and practices for purposes of world benefit. Constructionist theory and practice locates the source of meaning, value and action in communicative relations among people. Chief importance is placed on relational process and its outcomes for the welfare of all. Taos Institute Publications offers contributions to cutting-edge theory and practice in social construction. These books are designed for scholars, practitioners, students and the openly curious. The **Focus Book Series** provides brief introductions and overviews that illuminate theories, concepts and useful practices. The **Books for Professionals Series** provides in-depth works, focusing on recent developments in theory and practice. Books in both series are particularly relevant to social scientists and to practitioners concerned with individual, family, organizational, community and societal change.

Kenneth J. Gergen
President, Board of Directors
The Taos Institute

For information about the Taos Institute and social constructionism visit: www.taosinstitute.net.

Taos Institute Publications

Focus Book Series

The Appreciative Organization, Revised Edition (2008) by Harlene Anderson, David Cooperrider, Kenneth J. Gergen, Mary Gergen, Sheila McNamee, Jane Watkins, and Diana Whitney

Appreciative Inquiry: A Positive Approach to Building Cooperative Capacity, (2005) by Frank Barrett and Ronald Fry

Dynamic Relationships: Unleashing the Power of Appreciative Inquiry in Daily Living, (2005) by Jacqueline Stavros and Cheri B. Torres

Appreciative Sharing of Knowledge: Leveraging Knowledge Management for Strategic Change, (2004) by Tojo Thatchenkery

Social Construction: Entering the Dialogue, (2004) by Kenneth J. Gergen and Mary Gergen

Appreciative Leaders: In the Eye of the Beholder, (2001) edited by Marge Schiller, Bea Mah Holland, and Deanna Riley

Experience AI: A Practitioner's Guide to Integrating Appreciative Inquiry and Experiential Learning, (2001) by Miriam Ricketts and Jim Willis

Books for Professionals Series

Conversational Realities Reloaded: Baktin, Wittgenstein, and other New Studies in Social Construction, (2008) by John Shotter

Horizons in Buddhist Psychology: Practice, Research, and Theory, (2006) edited by Maurits G. T. Kwee, Kenneth J. Gergen, and Fusako Koshikawa

Therapeutic Realities: Collaboration, Oppression, and Relational Flow, (2005) by Kenneth J. Gergen

SocioDynamic Counselling: A Practical Guide to Meaning Making, (2004) by R. Vance Peavy

Experiential Learning Exercises in Social Construction — A Fieldbook for Creating Change, (2004) by Robert Cottor, Alan Asher, Judith Levin, and Cindy Weiser

Dialogues About a New Psychology, (2004) by Jan Smedslund

For online ordering of books from Taos Institute Publications visit
www.taosinstitutepublications.net.

For further information, call: 1-888-999-TAOS, 1-440-338-6733
email: info@taosinstitute.net.

Table Of Contents

Chapter 1

The Drama of
Social Construction

A dramatic transformation is taking place in the world of ideas. Everywhere traditions are thrown into question. There is growing doubt in universal and authoritative standards of truth, objectivity, rationality, progress, and morality. Faith is everywhere tested; insecurity raps incessantly at the door. Yet, from this tumultuous condition new dialogues are emerging; new voices of hope and promise for human existence are raised. These conversations now move across continents and cultures and are accompanied by a profusion of new professional practices — in organizations, education, therapy, social research, social work, counseling, conflict resolution, community development and more.

There are many names for this revolution in thought and practice. Terms such as post-foundationalism, post-empiricism, post-Enlightenment and postmodernism are often among them. However, woven through all these discussions is the notion of social construction — that is, the creation of meaning through our collaborative activities. While social construction is neither authored by any single individual or group, nor singular and unified, there is substantial sharing across communities. Tensions and insecurities are not feared because to establish a final truth, a foundational logic, a code of values or one slate of practices would be contrary to the very unfolding of ideas championed by social constructionists.

We authors have spent most of our professional careers engaged in constructionist dialogues. Our purpose in this book is to present an account that will enable students, colleagues and practitioners — as well as those who are simply curious — to gain a basic understanding and appreciation of the drama and power of these ideas. In the first two chapters we will outline some of the most important theoretical developments. We will then turn to the impact of such ideas on the ways we live and work. We shall be concerned with constructionist ideas in action — in organizations, psychotherapy, education, conflict resolution, social research, and everyday life. Finally we shall take up common critiques of constructionism. [1]

The Basic Idea: We Construct the World

Social constructionism is based on one major idea, simple and straightforward. However, as we unpack the implications and consequences, this simplicity will rapidly dissolve. The basic idea asks us to rethink virtually everything we have been taught about the world and ourselves. And with this rethinking we are invited into new and exciting forms of action.

To appreciate the possibilities, consider the world of common sense knowledge. What is more obvious than the fact that the world is simply out there for us to observe and understand? There are

[1] The term "constructivism" is often used interchangeably with "constructionism." Constructivism places the site of the world construction within the mind or interior of the individual. While there are certain commonalities between this movement and social constructionism, we will use the latter terms exclusively in the present work to underscore the central importance placed, not on individuals, but on relationships as the site of world construction.

trees, buildings, automobiles, women, men, dogs and cats, and so on. If we observe carefully enough, we can learn how to save the forests, build strong buildings, and improve the health of children. Now, let's stand these trusted assumptions on their head.

What if we said there are no trees, buildings, women, men and so on until we agree that there are? "Absurd," you may say, "Just look around you; all these were here long before we came along." That sounds reasonable, but let's take little Julie, a one-year-old, out for a walk. Her gaze seems to move past trees, buildings and cars without notice; she does not seem to distinguish men from women. William James once said that the world of a child is a "booming, buzzing confusion." Whether you agree with him or not, Julie's world doesn't seem to be the kind we live in as adults.

Unlike Julie, we notice autumn leaves turning from green to gold, that the house on our left is Victorian, the car in the street is a BMW, and that the woman standing in that door is actually a transvestite. What reaches our eyeballs may not be different from Julie's, but what this world means to us is different. We construct the world in a different way. This difference is rooted in our social relationships. From these relationships the world has become what it is.

Different You's from Different Views

Let's take you, the reader as the object of our lesson. Who or what are you? Imagine that you are standing in front of a large group of people, drawn from all walks of life and regions of the world. Each person looks at you and then announces what he/she sees before them. It might go like this:

To the:	You are:
Biologist	"a mammal"
Hairdresser	"last year's style"
Teacher	"promising"
Gay man	"straight"
Fundamentalist Christian	"a sinner"
Parent	"surprisingly successful"
Artist	"an excellent model"
Psychologist	"slightly neurotic"
Physicist	"an atomic composition"
Banker	"a future customer"
Doctor	"a hypochondriac"
Hindu	"imperfect state of Atman"
Lover	"a wonderful person"
Ifalukian	"filled with liget"

If there were no one to identify you, what then would you be? Would you be anything at all?

The foundational idea of social construction seems simple enough, but it is also profound. Everything we consider real is socially constructed. Or, more dramatically, *Nothing* is real unless people agree that it is.

Your skeptical voice might respond, "You mean that death is not real," or "the body," or "the sun," or "this chair" ... and the list goes on. We must be clear on this point. Social constructionists do not say, "There is nothing," or "There is no reality." The important point is that whenever people define what "reality" is, they are always speaking from a cultural tradition. To be sure, something has happened for them, but to describe it will require that it be represented from a particular cultural standpoint — in a particular language, or through some visual or oral media.

To illustrate, if we say, "His father died," we are usually speaking from a biological standpoint. We are constructing the event as the termination of certain bodily functioning. (Yet even medical specialists may disagree on the definition of death; the transplant surgeon may have a different opinion from the family physician.) From other traditions we might also say, "He has gone to heaven," "He will live forever in her heart," "This is the beginning of a new cycle of his reincarnation," "His burden has been eased," "He lives in his legacy of good works," "In his three children, his life goes on," or "The atomic composition of this object has changed." Outside all conventions of understanding, what is there to be said? For little Julie, the event might indeed be unremarkable. For the constructionist, it is not that, "There is nothing," but "nothing for us." In other words, it is from our relationships that the world becomes filled with what we take to be "trees," "the sun," "bodies," "chairs" and so on.

In a broader sense, we may say that as we communicate with each other we construct the world in which we live. If we remain in our familiar traditions, life may continue as usual. As long as we make the familiar distinctions, for example, between men and women, the rich and the poor or the educated and the uneducated, life remains relatively predictable. Yet, all that we take for granted can also be challenged. For example, "problems" don't exist in the world for all to see; rather we construct worlds of "the good" and deem those events that stand in the way of achieving what we value as "a problem." Could all that we construct as "problems" not be reconstructed as "opportunities?" By the same token, as we speak together, we could also bring new worlds into being. We could construct a world in which there are three genders or a world where the "mentally ill" are "heroes," or where "the power in all organizations lies not within individual leaders but in relationships."

It is at this point that you can begin to appreciate the enormous potential of constructionist ideas. For the constructionist, our actions are not constrained by anything traditionally accepted as true, rational, or right. Standing before us is a vast spectrum of possibility, an endless invitation to innovation. This is not to say that we should, then, abandon all that we take to be real and good. Not at all. But it is to say that we are not bound by the chains of either history or tradition. As we speak together, listen to new voices, raise questions, ponder alternative metaphors, and play at the edges of reason, we cross the threshold into new worlds of meaning. The future is ours — together — to create.

Positive Aging: A Case Study

Typically we view aging as a period of decline. As commonly understood, childhood is a period of development, in adulthood we reach maturity, and in old age we go down hill. But consider this commonplace construction. We live our adult years with a dread of aging; we look relentlessly for ways to "stay young," or at least "to look young." Old is bad. And for many, the view of decline is also self-fulfilling. Because "I am getting old, I must cut down on my activities, exercise and interests." As a result, the body and one's enthusiasm for life decline.

But if aging is a social construction, why should we sustain the negative understanding? Aren't there ways in which we could see aging as a positive process, a period of growth, enrichment and development? Challenged by this possibility, the two of us have created an electronic newsletter called Positive Aging. Here we include diverse materials from scientific research and elsewhere that emphasizes the positive potentials of aging. Readers everywhere seem pleased. As one reader said, "The newsletter keeps up my hopes that I will continue to have a fulfilling life for a long time."

Most enlightening for us have been workshops we have conducted with people interested in positive aging. Here we challenge groups to develop positive reconstructions for such dreaded events as "physical decline," "chronic illness," "loss of physical attractiveness" and "loss of loved ones." In general, such groups are wonderfully creative. They show us, for example, that chronic illness is also an opportunity for appreciating the significance of loved ones, for learning patience and tolerance, for dropping pretenses, for having time to learn and explore and for creating new avenues of activity (for example, making a family web-site, starting support groups, learning a new skill or writing poetry.) These groups teach us that together we may produce new realities of aging.

From Language Games to Possible Worlds

The basic idea of social construction is both simple and challenging. Further dimensions are revealed as we explore the broader reach of constructionist ideas. We begin with a focus on language, but as we shall find, our concerns rapidly broaden to include all forms of cultural life.

Language: From the Picture to the Practice

Where knowledge is concerned we have long treated language as a form of picture. When scientists tell us about the world, we expect their words to be accurate portrayals of their observations. In the same way we search for news reports that give an accurate depiction of events. While this seems obvious enough, consider again. Take the simple process of naming. There is Frank, Sally, Ben and Shawn. Now these individuals were scarcely born into the world with nametags. Their parents assigned their names. In this sense, they are arbitrary. Except perhaps for family traditions, for example, Frank could have been named Ben, Robert, Donald or something else. But why were they given names in the first place? The most important reason is practicality. For example, parents want to talk about Sally's welfare; is she eating properly, does her diaper need changing, is her brother Frank jealous of her? In effect, the parents require the name to carry out practices of good parenting; and later they will need the name for other practical purposes, like enrolling her in school and asking why she is out so late. More broadly, the words we use — just like the names we give to each other — are used to carry out relationships. They are not pictures of the world, but practical actions in the world.

This is easy enough to understand in the case of words like "Stop," "Danger!" or "Throw me the ball." And you can begin to see how our use of common names is socially useful. However, it is less obvious in the case of news reports, scientific accounts or telling someone about your day. Here the words seem to function like pictures, and they can be checked for accuracy. But consider again: *whether an account seems "accurate" will depend on a communal tradition.* Recall the example of the many "you's" earlier in the chapter. Each tradition has its own criteria of judgment. Thus, whether we think a witness in a trial is telling the truth depends on whether he or she uses language the same way we do. Whether "developers" are creating new neighborhoods or destroying open spaces depends upon what one means by "develop." In this sense, to "speak the truth" is to speak in a way that supports a particular community's traditions.

Language Games and the Limits of Our World

The famous philosopher, Ludwig Wittgenstein, introduced the metaphor of the language game. The metaphor enabled him to show how the words we use are embedded within systems of rules or shared conventions. This is easy enough to see in the case of grammar. Common rules will not allow us to say, "she go in beach," or "ball hit he." However, in any culture there are many different language games, that is, local conventions for describing and explaining. And, when you participate in the local convention, your freedom

15

of speech is radically limited. For example, in the case of the different "you's", each group relies on a different language game. Biologists are immersed in different language games from physicists, bankers or priests. When they come to describe you, they each play by different rules. Each makes good sense within his or her game. But to enter any of these cultures and play by different rules is perilous. You can scarcely ask a biologist about the soul of a frog, or a hairdresser about the atomic composition of a curl, without raising questions about your sanity.

Yet, we are not dealing here with the rules for language alone. Words are typically embedded in our activities, in the way we move or dress, or the objects we carry and what we do with them. In the game of chess, for example, we speak of "pawns," "rooks," "checkmate" and so on. Yet, you cannot simply walk down the street shouting, "Checkmate!" without raising a few eyebrows. The sentence only makes sense when people are carrying out certain prescribed activities using prescribed objects. This is also to say that the words we use inform people of the actions they should take. If we point to an object and call it a "chair," you may feel no reservations in taking a seat; if we call it a "precious antique," you will probably sit somewhere else. For the constructionist, then, we are invited into a double listening: for content and for consequence.

In Wittgenstein's terms our "language games," are embedded in broader patterns of activity that he called *forms of life*. In effect, biologists, hairdressers and bankers are engaged in different forms of life. Words help to hold their different forms of life together, and the forms of life simultaneously give the words their significance.

16

At the same time, these forms of life begin to form the limits of our worlds.

The Real as the Good

All of us are taught the difference between facts and values. We learn that facts are the "hard stuff," statements of evidence — objective and unbiased by desires, politics, religion and so on. In contrast, we learn that values are soft and subjective; they are without any solid foundation, simply representing the private investments of the individual. We should all agree on the facts; but everyone is entitled to their own values. *Social constructionism challenges this long-standing distinction.*

To appreciate the argument, consider three different newspaper headlines describing events when Saddam Hussein's Iraqi regime collapsed in 2003:

- U.S. Troops Victorious in Baghdad
- The American Empire Claims Victory in Iraq
- Iraqi Forces in Hiding as Americans Occupy Baghdad

Each of these headlines attempts to describe "what happened in Iraq," but they differ significantly in implications. The first, from an American paper, simply treats the Americans as victors. It is self-congratulatory. The second, reflecting the views of a Brazilian newspaper, uses the term "Empire" in derision, indicating that victory is only a claim. The future may prove otherwise. The final headline, reflecting views in some Arab countries, suggests that the "victory" is only a temporary "occupation;" Iraqi forces are hiding out within the civilian population, readied for return when the Americans depart. The events to which these stories refer may be identical. However, the description of "the facts" depends on the tradition in which one is writing. And each tradition carries with it its own values. All factual descriptions, then, sustain some tradition of value — for good or ill. In this sense, there are no value-free descriptions.

You may object, "Certainly the facts of the natural sciences are value neutral?" But consider again. Why do we accept the fact that medical science "cures" disease as unbiased? This is largely because we place a value on certain changes that doctors help to bring about in the body. This value is represented in the word, "cure;" if someone talked about the same actions of the profession as "interfering with nature's ways," we would see it as biased. In the same way, if you reduce the world to the language of physics, chemistry or biology, the language of "moral action" ceases to exist. If you continue to talk in scientific terms alone, dropping an atomic bomb on Nagasaki or conducting biological experiments with prisoners in concentration camps is not about "murder" or "morality." Such words are irrelevant to the science as such. And, in the same way, military forces may attack a country and simply talk about the thousands of civilians who are killed as "collateral damage." The natural sciences do have values; they analyze data in ways that allow them to achieve the ends of prediction and control; their discourses are tied to these purposes. If one remains solely within a given tradition, other traditions of value are simply irrelevant or suppressed.

Radical Pluralism

Most people are willing to agree that many of our categories are socially constructed. We all know that there are interminable disagreements on what constitutes "justice," "morality" or "love." However, many people resist constructionist ideas when it comes to the physical world, the pre-linguistic world of the directly observable. Is it true or false that the moon is made of blue cheese? How foolish to answer, "true." And isn't it equally obvious that the world is round and that the seasons in New England change? But consider again: if what we take to be real derives from communal agreement, then claims to truth must be located within these relationships. Or, to repeat, truth is only found within community. Beyond community there is silence. In this sense, social constructionists do not embrace universal truths, or Truth with a capital T, sometimes called Transcendental Truth.

To be sure, there is truth with a small t, that is, truth that issues from the shared ways of life within a group. Sometimes that group can be huge, as in the group that usually states that $2 + 2 = 4$. If a child says the answer was 3, correction soon follows. Mathematicians could say, however, that 4 is only true as long as the base of the mathematical system is 10. If it were otherwise, the answer would not be 4. The division of people into two sexes, male and female, is commonly accepted. However, there are some cultures that construct a third sex, intermediate between female and male. The notion of races is also one developed within communities and in some cultures, classes or caste systems have divided the higher

19

and lower social positions. So, to return to the question of whether the moon is made of blue cheese or something else, the answer depends upon the community in which we are engaged. In a poetic frame we might even say the moon is the ancient goddess, Diana.

The idea of truth within community is of enormous consequence. As we have seen, all constructions of the real are embedded within ways of life, and all ways of life are value invested. This means that claims to truth are invariably wedded to traditions of value. Thus, it is important within a community of rocket scientists to know whether it is true or false that a rocket will follow a certain trajectory; this truth is wedded to the value they place on safely reaching a destination. Psychiatrists attempt to know the truth about mental illness; this search is tied to the values they place on what they consider normal ways of life.

Our troubles begin, however, when local claims to truth (t) are treated as transcendental truth (T), when one community claims that the world was created by a Big Bang and another by a Big God, when one claims that homosexuality is a disorder and another that it is a normal human activity, or one claims that all behavior is determined and another that people have free will. Like most claims to knowledge, the humility of the local is replaced by the arrogance of the universal.

Social constructionism frees us from the task of trying to decide which tradition, set of values, religions, political ideologies, or ethics is ultimately or transcendentally True or Right. From a constructionist perspective, all may be valid for some group of people. Constructionist ideas invite a radical pluralism, that is, an openness to many ways of naming and valuing. Because there is no foundation for claiming superiority of one's own tradition, one is invited into a posture of curiosity and respect for others. What do other traditions offer that are not contained in one's own, what can be shared of our own that may be of value to others?

Of course, a pluralist view such as this is easier to espouse in the abstract than in the hurly burly of everyday life. We can scarcely rest silent in the face of what we see as the prejudice, oppression, injustice and brutality in today's world. However, for the constructionist, the inclination to stamp out what we despise is a move in the wrong direction. It is Truth in operation. Rather, the constructionist is more likely to favor forms of dialogue out of which new realities and values might emerge. The challenge is not to locate "the one best way," but to create the kinds of relationships in which we can collaboratively build our future. We shall say more about such relationships in Chapter 3.

Science vs. Religion?

Most scientists believe that there is a real, material world, independent of people; that it is possible to discover that world through systematic measurement (telescopes, microscopes, etc.); and, that it is possible to represent that world accurately through symbolic systems, including language and mathematical formulas. Scientists usually argue that through their methods they are able to come to closer and closer approximations to the world as it truly is. The successes that scientific enterprises have achieved, from the eradication of fatal diseases to the harnessing of atomic energy, have lead many to accept the power of science to reveal the Truth about the world.

Constructionist ideas do not at all devalue the scientific enterprise, but they do challenge the idea that science reveals Truth. Nor do the fruits of science justify any such claims. An effective practice of therapy, for example, does not render True the words that are used in describing or explaining the practice. This is an important point because for several hundred years claims to scientific Truth has been used to discredit the claims of religious or spiritual traditions. Science has served as a wedge in a power struggle in which societal control has been wrested away from religious institutions. Science deals in truth, it is said, where religious and spiritual traditions are based on fantasy or myth.

Constructionism provides a new way of seeing this antagonism: Scientific and religious/spiritual traditions each have their own ways of constructing the world; each harbors certain values and favor certain ways of life. There is no comparing the truth of these traditions against the truth of science directly. Any such measurement would necessarily take place within the constructed reality of some tradition. We cannot measure the truth of the spirit through scientific means any more than we can assess the truth of science through a spiritual sensitivity. And too, both traditions bring forth fruits in their own terms — rockets to the moon and atomic power in the former case, for example, and institutions of humane concern and visions of the moral good in the latter. Neither, within its own terms, can produce what the other offers. Constructionism asks us to eliminate the traditional opposition: Science vs. Religion.

Rather, we move to a position of both/and, where we are invited to explore from many standpoints both the positive and negative consequences of each.

Summary Focus

We may view social constructionism as a continuing dialogue on the sources of what we take to be knowledge of the real, the rational, the true, and the good — in effect, all that is meaningful in life. You may find it useful here to think of constructionist ideas as an umbrella under which all traditions of meaning and action are sheltered. The constructionist umbrella allows us to move across the traditions, to appreciate, evaluate, absorb, amalgamate and recreate. At the same time, constructionist ideas themselves must be given a place under the umbrella. They too must avoid claims to transcendent Truth. As we write these words, we are also striving to generate meaning together with you, the reader. The important question is not whether our words are true or objective, but rather what happens to our lives when we enter this form of understanding? As we shall hope to show, many new and promising pathways stand before us.

Chapter 2

From Critique to Reconstruction

One of the most fascinating things about our own engagement with constructionist ideas is the unceasing creativity they invite. Seekers of Truth attempt to reduce the world to a singular, fixed set of words. To declare The Truth is to set language into a deep freeze, and thus reduce the realm of possibilities for new meanings to emerge. In contrast, constructionists favor an ever-open dialogue, in which there is always room for another voice, another vision and revision, and further expansion in the field of relationship. In this chapter we introduce several major developments in the constructionist dialogues. We first take up the constructionist contribution to critical reflection. This discussion prepares us to consider the sweeping challenge constructionist ideas pose to the Western tradition of individualism. As we find, constructionism favors a replacement of the individual as the source of meaning with the relationship. Finally, and more positively, we explore recent attempts to reconstruct the concept of the self.

Deconstruction and Beyond

As constructionist ideas have become increasingly widespread, so has critical reflection on our everyday lives. Why is this so? Because the moment we become aware that any pronouncement on the nature of things — regardless of the status, achievements or apparent genius of the speaker — is only "one way of putting things," we also realize that it could be otherwise. Each way of constructing the world sustains certain traditions — loaded with their particular values — while simultaneously disregarding all that is not included. We thus become curious about whose traditions in particular are honored or unquestioned, and whose voices are silent or suppressed? We start to ask, for example, what kind of world is constructed by this news report, that political speech, or a body of scientific writing? Who is favored; who is marginalized? Do we necessarily want to embrace this way of constructing the world and the future it will create for us? Such critical sensitivity is increasingly widespread in Western culture. We are becoming more sensitive to the ways in which television constructs various groups — African Americans, women, Italians, the elderly and so on. Media literacy programs sensitize us to the way "facts are spun" by politicians and how political ideology is subtly embedded within news reporting. Parents are widely concerned with the consumer attitudes that television teaches their children. All these considerations represent a critical stance toward the worlds constructed by others. In this sense, constructionist scholarship simply expresses a broad sensitivity already in motion.

Within the academic sphere, this critical orientation has become acutely sharpened. Feminist scholars have been especially prominent in such work. Early contributions made us all aware of the subtle biases inherent in such words as "mankind," "policeman," and "chairman;" many now ask why God is depicted as male.

Feminist scholars are now joined by numerous other groups who feel the oppressive weight of mainstream culture bearing down on their ways of life. Much of this critical work is now found in African American Studies, Asian Studies, Queer Studies, Cultural Studies, and more. In the next chapter we will explore the specific work of the "critical education" movement.

Which Has the Power: The Sperm or the Egg?

A powerful example of feminist critical work is found in Emily Martin's study of how medical texts describe the process of human fertilization. She notes that most popular descriptions follow a fairy tale form in which multitudes of active sperm (the heroic figures of the story) strive against great odds to capture the fortress and penetrate the Princess-Egg. Meanwhile, the princess sits passively waiting for the lucky, plucky winner of the contest. Fertilization is the successful end of the hero's conquest. As Martin points out, this biological account of fertilization adds scientific authority to the longstanding cultural myth of the powerful, active male and the passive, helpless female.

Of course, if we look at a video of the fertilization process, we virtually see the active sperm penetrating the passive egg. Or, do we? What would we see, asks Martin, if our story featured an exotic egg-siren who lures the helpless, hapless sperm into her lair? As she beckons them toward her, she selects one and destroys the rest. Here the egg becomes the dominating force. Our view of what is happening on the video changes accordingly.

To be sure, the second story is no more true than the first. (And no more politically correct!) They are both narrative constructions of what is taking place. However, the scientific implications are wholly different. For Martin, a medical anthropologist, it is especially important that we realize the political nature of our interpretations. The result is also better biology. In traditional research on infertility, attention was primarily paid to the mobility and the strength of the sperm. By adopting the second story — the egg as siren — attention is paid to the characteristics of the egg as well as to the passageway through which the sperm travels. Both stories, however, are limited. Might other narratives or metaphors be fruitful in enhancing our understandings of human reproduction?

Such critical endeavors are enormously important to the development of democracy. They thwart the attempt of any group to dominate or suppress others through their particular construction of the real and the good. They multiply the "checks and balances" in society that ensure full participation. For example, from the realization that all major newspapers report the news from a particular standpoint and that there are very few independent newspapers, hundreds of websites and Internet forums now enrich the possibilities for public expression. In addition to fostering democracy, many see such critical work as liberating. It is when people can see the limits and biases inherent in the otherwise taken for granted that they are freed to consider alternatives.

Yet, while essential for a just society, the critical impulse is also dangerous. Critique calls into question the legitimacy of what is said or written. And if it is your words that are under attack, then you may be revealed as prejudiced, self-serving, oppressive or exploitative. Unsurprisingly, the reaction to critique is often anger and counter-attack. Both the critic and the target typically believe in the good of what they are doing. Soon the possibility of trust is destroyed, and mutual hostility prevails. In this respect, new forms of discourse are needed to replace the tradition of all-out critique. How can we critically reflect without demonizing? How can we move past the barriers of separated sense-making to build more promising futures together? We shall glimpse some possibilities in Chapter 3.

From the Individual to Relationship

What is more obvious than the fact that our social world is made up of separate individuals, each normally endowed with the capacity for conscious decision making? It is because of this obvious fact that we favor a democracy in which each adult citizen has the right to cast a vote, courts of law in which we hold individual actors responsible for their deeds, schools in which we evaluate each student's individual work, and organizations in which we subject individual workers to performance evaluations. It is largely for these reasons that we characterize Western culture as individualist.

Yet, for a constructionist, the obvious fact of "the individual as conscious decision maker" is not so obvious. Rather, we see this as only one way of constructing the world. In fact, the individualist orientation to social life is not so old historically (possibly three centuries), and it is *not* shared by the majority of people on earth. This does not make it wrong, but it does allow us to step out of the box and ask about its pros and cons. What do we gain from this particular way of constructing the world; what do we lose; what are the alternatives?

To be sure, there is much to be said in favor of individualism. For example, life is meaningful and important to many people because they feel they are loved, honored or valued for themselves. And for most of us there is no preferable alternative to democracy. At the same time, individualism has its downside. From an individualist standpoint we are invited to see the social world as made up of fundamentally isolated beings. We learn that we cannot penetrate the minds of others, so we cannot fully know or trust each other. Because we presume that everyone is out for himself or herself, we require moral training in caring for others. Self-regard becomes the pivotal dimension around which we live our lives, fearful that we may be scorned, seeking always to be better than others. In an individualist world, relationships take a back seat because they are treated as artificial contrivances, possibly time consuming, and essential only in cases where one is not self-sufficient.

It is at just this point that constructionist ideas take wing. If a particular construction of self or world works against our well-being, we are invited to develop alternatives. Indeed, from a constructionist perspective, relationships — not individuals — constitute the foundation of society. Let us expand on this possibility, not because a relational view is true, but because when we step into this construction we may invite new and possibly more promising forms of action.

Meaning as Coordinated Action

Traditionally we speak of meaning as residing in the heads of individuals. We presume that words are outward expressions of the inner workings of the mind. When we ask someone, "What do you mean by that?" we expect the speaker to clarify his or her private thoughts. This conception of meaning lies toward the center of the individualist tradition; it honors the individual as the source of all meaning. Yet, in addition to its individualist bias, it also generates an impossible problem of human understanding. If meaning is "inside the other's head," and the only clue to "what's going on there"

31

are verbal expressions, then we shall never be able to comprehend the other. We can never verify that we are correct, save through the other's outward expressions. Yet, these outward expressions leave us in the same quandary; how can we know what they mean? We then enter what scholars call a *hermeneutic circle*, an unending circle in which each answer simply creates another question. The most promising way to escape the circle is to abandon the construction of the "an inner world" where meaning is created. Let us not focus on the meaning within the head, but the way in which meaning is created in relationship. We move from the within to the between. How can we make sense of meaning as relational?

Consider the following four propositions:

1) *An individual's utterances in themselves possess no meaning.*

A man passes a woman on the street. He smiles and says, "Hi Anna." She fails to hear the greeting and passes in silence. What then has he said? To be sure, he has uttered two words. However, for all the difference it makes he might have chosen two nonsense syllables or said nothing at all. He cannot make meaning alone.

2) *The potential for meaning is realized through supplementary action.*

A person's utterances begin to acquire meaning when another responds, that is, when the other adds supplementary action. If Anna replies, "Oh, hi, good morning..." she has created his words as a greeting. To communicate at all is to be granted by others a privilege of meaning. If others do not treat one's utterances as communication (e.g., "That doesn't make any sense at all"), if they fail to coordinate themselves around the offering (e.g., "That's just stupid."), one hasn't made meaning.

To combine these first two proposals, we see that meaning resides within neither individual, but only in their relationship. Both the act and supplement must be coordinated in order for meaning to occur. Like a handshake, a kiss, or a tango, it takes at least two.

3) *Supplementary action itself requires a supplement.*

Any supplement functions twice, first in granting significance to what has preceded, and, second, as an action that also requires supplementation. In effect, the meaning it grants remains suspended until it too is supplemented. Consider a therapy client who speaks of her sense of helplessness; she finds herself unable to cope with an aggressive husband and an intolerable job situation. The therapist can create these as expressions of depression, by responding, "Yes I can see why you are depressed; tell me a little more." However, this supplement stands idle of meaning until the client provides a supplement. If the client simply ignores the statement, the therapist's words are denied significance. If she says, "I didn't say I was depressed; I am just angry!" she reduces the therapist's statement to an arrogant assertion. When she says, "Yes, I am horribly depressed...," depression becomes a reality for them to work on together. More broadly, it could be said that we live our lives dialogically. We make sense only by virtue of what has preceded, and what follows.

4) *Traditions grant us possibilities for meaning, but do not determine what must be.*

It is important to recognize that the words and actions upon which we rely to generate meaning together are largely borrowed from other times and other places. If someone approached you and began to utter a string of vowels, "ahhh, ehhhh, ooooo, uuuu..." you would surely be puzzled; perhaps you would search for the nearest exit. This individual's actions are not part of any coordinated sequences with which you are familiar. In effect, our capacity to make meaning together today relies on a history, often of many centuries duration. In this sense, we owe to traditions of coordination our capacities for being in love, supporting a just cause, or taking pleasure in our children's development. In each case we borrow from the treasures of past relationships.

But we are not determined by the past. Novel combinations of action/supplement are always in motion. Consider a lively conversation. For any expression there are dozens of possible and meaningful supplements. As the conversation continues the result will be an utterly unique creation. You can also see here the value of play. When we agree to play or "fool around," we say and do things that are not entirely conventional. Novel sequences are generated ... laughter abounds ... and new insights may even be created.

The Relational Self

What is it to be a human being; what is our fundamental nature? This is not a question we often ask ourselves because we more or less take it for granted that humans are creatures who possess the capacity for rational decision making, feeling emotion and desire, remembering past times, and so on. Yet, as mentioned earlier, such common sense beliefs have only become central in Western culture within the past several centuries. Consider that not until Rene Descartes' 17th century dictum, "I think, therefore I am" was it so obvious that we could think, or that thinking was central to one's being a person. The concept of "feelings" didn't develop until the 18th century. And in the meantime, other human qualities have disappeared. For example, we have more or less forgotten the importance of "melancholy," an emotional state once characterized by sullenness and outbreaks of violent anger. Melancholy was so obvious in the 17th century that Robert Burton could write a 500-page book on its causes and cures. "The soul" has been a fact about human nature for centuries, although today many regard it as a myth. Free will has been considered a unique virtue of persons for the last few centuries, but, for most scientists who hold a deterministic view of the universe, free will is an obvious fiction.

Mental Illness as Deficit Discourse

Are you being treated for depression; do you know a young person who has been diagnosed with attention deficit disorder? Increasingly, the answer to such questions is "yes." Yet, there were no mental disorders called depression or attention deficit disorder until the 20th century. Interestingly, in 1900, we had only a handful of terms that identified "mental" illnesses. By the year 2000, mental health professionals had "discovered" over 400 forms of mental illness. Mental illness is now one of the chief health expenditures in the U.S., and psycho-pharmaceuticals are a multi-billion dollar business. As the discourse of personal deficit gains scientific credibility and the deficits become public knowledge, so do we come to construct ourselves in these ways.

From a social constructionist perspective, mental illness is not simply "out there" waiting to be discovered. Rather, we construct certain actions as "illness" ... or not. A person who is "sad," or "blue" or "in the doldrums" need not be diagnosed as "ill." Rather, we think he might need a bit of support from friends or family, a bit of success and recognition, a new girlfriend, or time to overcome a loss. If we label the person as having a "clinical depression," we turn him over to a treatment that may lead to life-long dependency on anti-depressants. If we describe a child as "brimming with curiosity" or "needing a great deal of stimulation," we might find her more interesting things to do. If the same child is diagnosed with attention deficit disorder, she will very likely have Ritalin prescribed to her for many years. As social constructionists, we are sensitized to these problematic effects of deficit discourse, and encourage the search for alternative constructions of greater promise.

Let us focus on the taken-for-granted world of mental activity we share today. Surely, to speak of our thoughts, feelings, desires and memories is enormously valuable to us. For example, what would an intimate relationship be if we didn't believe we were sharing our innermost feelings? Yet, simply because the ways we construct the mind are important to us does not place them beyond reflection. Consider that all these words — thought, emotion, desire, memory — construct a world "inside the head" of the individual. As we discussed in the Relational Self section, when the "inner world" is the most central feature of what it is to be a human being, we create a world of separation, isolation and conflict. We are unable to explain how communication is possible at all. Essentially, in our construction of the person we have contributed to an ideology of individualism, and its implications for social life are not altogether satisfying.

For the constructionist, such problems also form challenges to reconstruction. Is it possible, the constructionist asks, to reconstruct the "mental world" in such a way that it is no longer private, "in here," "behind the eyes?" Can we begin to regard thoughts, feelings, desires, memories and the like, as born in relationships, and as meaningless outside of relationships? If we were successful in our reconstruction, we would no longer see ourselves as isolated and independent, fundamentally self-seeking or endangered by competing others. We would see ourselves as a relational outcome. "Self vs. other" would become "self through other." Let us consider, then, some important steps toward the construction of the relational self.

The Relational Reconstruction of the Mind

The task of creating the relational self is not easy primarily because the words available to us are the products of an individualist tradition. We have thousands of terms that "make real" the conditions and contents of the individual mind. We can speak endlessly of our thoughts, feelings, desires, hopes, dreams, ideals, and so on. In contrast we have very few words for describing relationships. It's as if we have an enormously rich language to describe the pieces on a chessboard, but few to describe the game. How can we proceed to make sense of a relational self without starting with the assumption of individual minds? Many scholars are attempting now to answer this question.

Consider here four propositions that begin to open the door:

1) *The discourse of the mind is born in dialogue.*

Many believe that our words for mental states are required by the factual existence of the states themselves. That is, because thought actually exists in the head, we have come to develop the word, "thought." In contrast, the constructionist might argue that we don't have the word "thinking" because we have somehow peered into our minds and identified a process that we now call "thought." After all, what would we be looking at, as we can't see thoughts in our brains, and how would we identify a "thought" as opposed to an "attitude" or a "hope" even if we could?

Rather, our languages are born within our dialogues with others. Descartes' pronouncement about his "thinking" is only sensible within a particular history of dialogue. As he was talking to other philosophers, what if they had said, "What on earth do you mean by the word 'think'?" Without human coordination the utterance stands empty. Because our words for the mind are created in dialogue, it is easy to see why terms come and go in history, and why it is easy enough for us to invent hundreds of terms for mental illness. It also explains why the many cultures of the world do not share the same understanding of "what makes people tick."

2) *The discourse of mind acquires its value through its use.*

To say that the discourse of the mind is born in dialogue is also to say that its meaning depends on its social use. We don't need to ask, then, whether the words we use accurately portray our internal states. If you say, "I want you here with me very much," the question is not whether the word "want" matches a condition in your brain. Rather, the question is how these words function within a relationship. What are the social consequences of your saying these words?

Consider all the terms we have to express states of attraction. You can say, "I admire you," "I just want to be your friend," "You are great," "I like you," "I am fascinated by you," "I love you," "I adore you," "I am crazy about you," "I am desperate for you," and so on. The possibilities are almost countless. Now consider the impact on others when you use one of these phrases as opposed to another. Depending on when and with whom you say these words, others may come close, remain suspended, or even take out a restraining order against you! We have countless ways of talking about attraction, not because there are countless states of mind, but because of the demands of a complex life of relationships.

3) *Language is only one component of fully performed actions.*

So far we have placed a heavy emphasis on words alone — words such as thought, emotion, and so on. Clearly, however, such words are accompanied by facial expressions, posture, bodily movement and other activities. These bodily actions are vital to the way in which the words will function. You might say to someone, "I am so sorry I hurt you." However, if this utterance was accompanied by a laugh or a sneer, you might quickly find yourself in trouble. To sustain the relationship, a serious facial expression is required. It is useful here to think of actors who must create compelling performances of emotion — of love, anger, or compassion. Their words are only one component of the full bodily performance. They are not asking themselves about their true feelings; they are simply engaged in *the doing* of these emotions.

It is important to note that we are not saying that the "performances" are either superficial or calculating. When we are in "the heat of anger," for example, we are more fully engaged than the actor on the stage. In contrast, the actor must hold the performance at a distance; he or she must "play" the part as opposed to "be" the part. In the same way a basketball player leaps with intensity through the scramble of bodies to sink the basket, so can we "perform" our feelings with unswerving immersion. Nor unlike the actor, do we necessarily calculate the effects of our performances. One does not typically carry out two performances at once, on the one hand announcing, "I really do appreciate your help," and on the other, saying to oneself, "If I say this he will help me again." To be sure, such double performances are possible. But for the most part we are simply "there," performing authentically.

4) *Performances are components of relational sequences.*

The sense of a word depends significantly on the sentence in which it is embedded. The meaning of "ball" depends altogether on whether you say, "Throw the ball," as opposed to "We had a ball!" In the same way, performances of thinking or feeling are only sensible at specific points in a relational sequence. You cannot run up to a stranger and shout, "I am damned angry" and make cultural sense. However, if the stranger was trying to run away after denting the door of your car, the same expression might make perfect sense. Here we might even disapprove of the person who did not express anger. There are only certain times and places where an expression is relationally appropriate; otherwise it is simply weird.

It is useful here to think of dance — of swing, tango, or salsa. The movements of the dancers make sense only within the confines of the dance; neither partner alone can perform them. The movements of both partners are required to bring about the dance. Further, to be successful, the movement of each partner must be coordinated with the other. There are no purely solo movements. And too, certain movements are required at certain times — as when one partner signals the other to prepare to twirl in a swing dance.

In the same way, performances of the mind make sense only within certain relationships, they are expected at certain times within the relationship and not others, and they require the cooperation of the other to make sense. Thus, if a friend complements you, this action sets the stage for you to express pleasure (or embarrassment). And if you say something like, "Oh, that makes me very happy," you set the stage for a confirming reply, like, "You really deserve it." Each action invites the next; each requires the other for its legitimacy. More broadly, our performances of the mind are not our private possessions. They are components of relationship.

Pain as a Relational Event

Pain is pain, regardless of how you talk about it. Or so we believe. One of the most exciting implications of a relational view of mental discourse is that pain may not be such a personal event after all. Rather, how we experience pain may depend on the history and context of relationships. Consider the football player who emerges from the game bruised and bloody, and proclaiming, "I had a great time!" Then there is the sexual masochist who pays the dominatrix to beat him with a whip, and the Christian penitents of the Middle Ages who beat themselves in order to approach the pain of Christ on the cross. To be sure, there is a special physical sensation in all these cases, but whether we approach it as "awful pain," or "a welcome experience" depends on a culture of relationships.

Enormous amounts are spent each year on pain management. Most of these efforts presume that pain is pain, and that pain reduction must primarily depend on altering brain chemistry. Yet, from a constructionist standpoint, the more important question is whether we can reconstruct pain and embed the experience in new and more promising relational forms. In his groundbreaking book, The Wounded Storyteller, Arthur Frank proposes that our experience of pain vitally depends on the narratives by which it is understood. For example, in the *restitution narrative* ("before I had no pain; now I have terrible pain, but soon it will be over"), the pain ultimately gives way to a state of well-being. In this narrative, the pain is simply an undesirable irritant. One is miserable until normalcy is returned. The story of menstrual cramps is a typical restitution narrative. More promising, however, is the *quest narrative*. Here one sees oneself as on a mission toward greater understanding, perhaps spiritual enlightenment. Suffering enables one to be a witness, to inform others from a standpoint of wisdom. Now misery acquires positive meaning. The pains of labor in childbirth may be the ultimate example of the quest narrative. Pain, wisdom and joy are inextricably entwined.

Taking this relational view, we can reconstruct all we have presumed to be personal, private and "in the head" events — thoughts, emotions, plans, desires, and so on — as fundamentally relational. To feel sadness or joy, ecstasy or agony, love or hate, desire or loathing is to take part in the tradition of relationship. We do not possess these states inside of us; they are not locked into brain structures; rather we actively perform them. They are not moving us to action, nor is our action stimulating them into life. The states and the action are one and the same.

Your skeptical voice might reply, "But I do have private experience; I often think or have emotions when I am totally alone." Let us consider: we may be cut away from others in terms of our bodies. But the activities in which we engage alone are very much wedded to our immersion in relationships. Our activities of "feeling sad" or "thinking about a problem" are essentially partial performances, cut away from the normal circumstances of relationship. To "think to oneself," in this sense, is like carrying out a public conversation, only without the full performance of talking with another person. To feel sad in the privacy of one's room is not essentially different from performing sadness publicly. However, alone we may not "do it fully" — with appropriate facial expressions and body posture. Sitting alone and feeling sad is taking part in the cultural dance but without others present. Without a history of relationship there is little to be called "a private world."

Summary Focus

The present chapter extends consideration and appreciation for relational processes. It is out of relationship that all we take to be real, rational, true and valuable emerge. The implications of a relational emphasis are substantial. Not only do we unsettle the deep-seated tradition of individualism, we are also invited to reconsider many of our institutions, from our intimate rituals of relationship to our practices of education, politics and law. A relational perspective kindles a keen appreciation of our life with others, not set apart from or against them. We begin to center on the generative power of relationship and the flow of coordinated actions. Through performances with others as well as with ourselves, we create our rational and emotional realities. What was previously called "mental processes" becomes recreated as "relational processes." It is the "relational self" which comes into being through relationships with others. In the next two chapters we explore practices in organizations, schools, therapy and research that carry relational conceptions into action.

Chapter 3

Social Construction and Professional Practice

It is one thing to generate attractive ideas; the important question is whether there is a productive relationship between the words and our ways of life. The two of us have spent most of our careers as academics. We have witnessed many interesting ideas come and go. However, one of the reasons we have been especially drawn to constructionist ideas is that they do make important differences in our lives. Once consciousness of construction sets in, it is difficult to sit still. For example, when you realize that all we take to be true, rational and good is only so by virtue of convention, you begin to ask questions of unsettling significance. Why must we accept what tradition has dished onto our plate; what are we missing; could we reconstruct; would it be better? The questions are provocative; the repercussions endless.

In this chapter, we discuss the impact of constructionist ideas on professional practices. We illustrate developments in the professions of therapy, organizational development, teaching and conflict resolution — all professions specifically engaged in human change. In each of these areas constructionist ideas have encouraged new and exciting courses of action.

Social Construction and Therapeutic Change

Working to alleviate individual suffering is no easy matter, and the search for "the best form of therapy" has been unceasing. One of the benefits of a constructionist perspective is that one can stop searching for the perfect solution and appreciate that there are "different strokes for different folks." For clients and therapists, alike, ways of doing therapy should be sensitive to personal styles and preferences, to differing traditions and values — in effect, to the multiple constructions of the real and the good. Therapeutic traditions are themselves pockets of cultural meaning; why should there be a single meaning system useful for all people? That said, three forms of therapy are especially congenial with the constructionist sensitivity to multiple realities; each offers important resources for change.

Narrative Therapy: Re-Storying Lives

We understand our lives largely in terms of stories in which we are the main character. These may be stories about growing up, falling in love, finding a career path, and so on. They are stories of success and failure, of doing good and less than good. Who would we be if we had not stories? Thus, when an individual suffers from a problem in living, this problem is only sensible from within some kind of story. We often suffer, for example, when we confront a loss, when we have been rejected, or when we feel we have no direction in life. But loss, rejection, and being rudderless in life are not "problems out there in nature." They can only take place from within a story plot. For you to "lose" something (a job, a close friend, the love of others) means that you carry around a story of yourself as a major character, embarked on a course of progress or fulfillment (end-points of a good story), and have suffered a setback.

Narrative therapists have a keen appreciation of these ideas, and believe that through "re-storying" one's life, "problems" can be transformed; new stories can be constructed, and from these, new courses of action can be opened. For example, some people carry with them a story in which they were permanently damaged by abusive parents. They feel unable to move forward. However, if they can revisit the early years with an eye toward how they intrepidly survived — emerging as a hero — they may begin to see new and more optimistic options for action.

The challenging work of family therapists, Michael White and David Epston focuses especially on the political potentials of re-storying. Most people see their problems as residing "in their heads." They feel personally dysfunctional. As White and Epston reason, such narratives obscure the possibility of understanding one's problems as issuing from the socio-political conditions. What we often take to be personal dysfunctions — such as depression — can be re-storied so that we can see that we are confronting stressful economic or political conditions. When one understands that "it is not me, but the system," a layer of self-doubt is removed and new courses of action are invited. For example, White helps the Aboriginal people of Australia see personal distress as produced by external social conditions of oppression. In these relationships with powerful white people, they have come to feel dis-empowered.

This story of struggle with an outside force is strengthened by demonstrating the ways cultural forces are biased against them. By co-constructing stories of strength, individual distress is often reduced and political action invited.

Brief & Solution-Focused Therapies: Word Magic

Clients typically enter therapy with problems they wish to discuss. There are merits to such discussions, but there are also shortcomings. From a constructionist standpoint, when we talk in earnest about a problem, the problem becomes increasingly real and increasingly formidable. If we talk about it long enough, we may come to feel helplessly caught in its grip. Drawing from constructionist ideas, brief and solution-focused therapists search for alternatives to "problem talk," that is focused on the individual's, difficulties. Instead, they invite discussion of strengths, resources, and relational possibilities. Consider, for example, what is called "the miracle question." Here clients are asked, in effect, "What would it be like tomorrow if you woke up and the problem were no longer there?" The therapist then helps the clients to move in the direction their fantasy leads. Focusing on a positive future instead of a "bad old past" becomes the basis of more pro-active steps toward change.

Brief therapy is also interesting as a contrast to long-term therapies such as psychoanalysis. From a constructionist base, therapies such as psychoanalysis require years of probing because they construct the person as possessing "deep seated problems." If problems are defined as lurking in unconscious memories from early childhood, then many hours of therapy seem reasonable. However, we can also construct the individual in a different way, one that says we primarily live in the here and now, and our well being is importantly linked to our current relationships. If we take the latter position, then therapy can be far briefer (and less costly). Outcomes of therapy are also differently framed. Instead of probing the troubled past, therapy focuses on means toward more adequate relationships in the present. When one reconstructs from past to present, and from problems to potentials, more rapid change can be anticipated.

Postmodern Therapy and the "Not Knowing" Position

Traditional schools of therapy are based on the assumption of expert knowledge. That is, therapists are trained to recognize the causes and cures of people's problems ("illnesses"). Of course, what is "known" varies greatly from one school of therapy to another. Differing schools variously hold that the individual's problems are tied in with suppressed sexual desires, the lack of parental love, a sense of inferiority and so on. Notice that a therapist committed to one of these explanations knows about the client's problems before he or she walks in the door. Therapy from a "knowing position" doesn't give the client's "knowing" any credit.

Harry Goolishian and Harlene Anderson of the Houston-Galveston Institute for Family Therapy proposed an alternative, called a "not knowing" orientation. In this case the therapist is guided by an intense curiosity about what family members are saying and how they construct their world. Such therapists don't abandon all previous understanding, but rather, see past experiences as offering possible resources for enriching the therapeutic conversation. Most importantly, the therapist gains a sensitivity to the new meanings that might be constructed from the understandings clients bring with them into therapy. Change grows outward from the client's realities.

To illustrate, consider a family in which the father seems to be a tyrant. A "knowing" therapist might quickly conclude that he is expressing a personality disorder which is causing rebellious resistance among the family members. While this seems reasonable enough, the "not knowing" therapist would see this as only one possible interpretation. By curiously exploring the world in which this supposed tyrant lives, other potentials might well be revealed. For example, with continued probing the dad might reveal that he feels ashamed of his bad-temper and wishes he could express his loving feelings to his children more openly. With this shift in the conversation, therapy might be transformed. Rather than trying to understand why Dad has to be so mean, family members might find a more successful way of relating to him as he finds new ways to express himself.

From therapy practices, let us turn now to a second site of constructionist practice, the organization.

Social Construction and Organizational Efficacy

The success of any organization depends significantly on the capacity of its participants to negotiate meaning effectively. Teams cease to be effective when members are in conflict; leaders cease to lead when no one understands or appreciates what they say. It should be no surprise, then, that social constructionist ideas have been highly influential in organizational work.

Constructionist scholars have often stressed the ways in which organizations resemble small cultures and the way these cultures are tied together by shared assumptions of the real and the good. Of major importance in bringing a culture together are their narratives. Especially crucial are those narratives that create a collective sense of history and destiny. Most readers will recognize the power of family stories (e.g., Grandpa's antics, Mom's weird birthday cakes, the dog's misdeeds) in creating a sense of "our family." Organizations are much the same. Stories can suggest that with the kind of courage, ingenuity and hard work evidenced in the past, working together can bring about great accomplishments. Let us consider two more recent contributions of constructionist ideas to organizational practices.

From Individual to Relational Leadership

When you think of an outstanding leader, chances are you imagine a single individual — typically male — who is blessed with special skills, wisdom or powers of persuasion. Indeed, much traditional study of organizational leadership embraces the "Great Man" vision of the leader. From this perspective, leaders exert an influence over their followers, and effective leaders are those who inspire and direct in ways that bring about organizational success.

For constructionists, however, this view of leadership is deeply flawed. It fails to take into account the manner by which meaning is created in relationship. No one can function as a leader unless joined by others in the process of making meaning. Even when the leaders of the former Soviet Union controlled all the major institutions in the country, the government collapsed without conflict. The people did not accept reality as constructed on high. They had negotiated a different construction of their country's destiny. Sensitive to the co-construction of meaning and eager to improve the quality of life in organizations, theorists and practitioners are now drawn to new visions of leadership. They carve out concepts and practices in which leadership is a relational process.

One of the most influential accounts of relational leadership can be found in Wilfred Drath's, The Deep Blue Sea: Rethinking the Source of Leadership. Relational leadership emerges when people in dialogue create leadership roles and leadership activities among themselves. In Drath's words, leadership is understood, "not as a possession of the leader but as an aspect of the community" (pg. xvi). Rather than the single individual establishing visions and goals, these are shaped through dialogues among those involved. The task of leading becomes distributed among the participants.

It is useful here to think of the way in which a friendship group functions. In most cases all participants have a voice in what the group will do. They may place a member of the group in the position of "the leader" from time to time. Different friends will have different forms of expertise or special resources. However, continued negotiation is essential for the friendship to continue. The consequences of applying a relational perspective to leadership have revolutionary implications. For example, once the model of the leader as a single-minded visionary is abandoned, there will be more buy-in from the participants. They are not simply taking orders and dispassionately going through the day; rather, because they have a personal investment in policies and practices they are vitally engaged. Praise and blame will also be more evenly distributed. For example, today CEO's salaries, on average, are over 500 times greater than their average hourly worker's. This is the outcome of the individual hero model of leadership. If the CEO were considered a part of a complex relational process, salaries might be more evenly distributed, and CEO's would be less often blamed as well. Further, organizational ethics might be improved. It is when a few individuals behind closed doors can make decisions that malfeasance is likely to result. With broad dialogue, common conventions of honesty are more likely to prevail.

Relational Leadership at Work

Barbara Waugh is considered a visionary leader in today's computer business. She served as the recruiting manger at Hewlett-Packard for over 17 years, and now heads an initiative to bring Internet opportunities to the underdeveloped world. She is also a leader who brings a strong relational orientation to her work. We quote here from her book, The Soul in the Computer:

> *Without my personal and professional relationships inside and outside the company, virtually none of the things in my life would have been accomplished ... HP itself is a good example of the power of relationships. It was founded on a relationship of love and respect between two people. This is not the Hewlett company or the Packard company, but the Hewlett-Packard Company. The order was decided not by higher or lower, greater or lesser, but by the flip of a coin. And the company grew through hundreds of significant relationships. Not just relationships with peers, but also relationships up and down the hierarchy....*

> *We cannot make or keep good relationships unless we listen. And listening wholly without preparing the next remark, without thinking about getting gas on the way home or whether our child did well on her math quiz. We must shut off the incessant "judgment machine" urging us to decide who's smarter, right, most likely to succeed. We must fall into each other's eyes. When we do this, magical things happen — things far greater than we could have imagined.* (pgs. 200-201).

Appreciative Inquiry: Inspiring Organizational Change

The organizational world abounds in "problem talk." One hears, "We have a problem with marketing," "Our CEO has no imagination," "The workers are unsatisfied," and so on. One imagines that if all the problems were solved the organization would run perfectly. But would it? If we focus on the individual problems we often lose sight of the whole; our eyes are no longer fastened on our vision for the future. We begin to find fault in each other; we become suspicious and defensive. The organizational dream always seems to be postponed as there is never an end to the problems that must be solved.

From a constructionist perspective, problem talk is *optional*. There are only problems if we construct the world in this way. And because problem talk often leads us away from our goals, we can ask whether there are other forms of talk more effective for the organization. In answer, one group of organizational specialists has given a hearty "yes!" This powerful means of mobilizing groups and organizations is called *Appreciative Inquiry*. Appreciative Inquiry (AI) is an alternative to problem-focused approaches to organizational change. AI practitioners create the world in ways that find the glass half-full instead of half-empty. As one of its creators, David Cooperrider, describes it, "The single most prolific thing a group can do, if it aims to consciously construct a better future, is to discover what the 'positive core' of any system is, and then make it the common and explicit property of all." Thus, Cooperrider stresses a focus on the most central strengths and resources of an organization, as opposed to its problem areas.

In exploring the positive core of the human system, the greater the participation of all group members, the better, deeper, more lasting the change process. In AI the relational realities of the group are discovered. It is through dialogue and conversation that new relationships are formed, and it is through the relationships that the future of the organization begins to emerge. In a typical AI session, members of the organization are paired off and asked to share stories that draw from this positive core. Participants discover those moments in organizational life when things were at their best. Typically these stories are about experiences in the organization from which the participants derived fulfillment, energy and joy. For example, the stories might be about some successful project in which the storyteller played a part, or a project in which participants were most enthusiastic. The stories are then shared in larger groups, with the ultimate aim of extracting from them the elements of the organization that give it life, vitality and strength.

From this sharing, the participants begin to discuss the future of the organization and how they can maximally tap these reservoirs of vitality. With a new, compelling vision in place, participants then set in motion plans to bring about the desired changes. The entire collaborative process typically ignites enthusiasm and good will and a resolve to accomplish great deeds. Importantly, AI locates the roots of the future within grounds of the past; the participants don't just share pipe dreams, but use the best of their past achievements to generate realistic and idealistic possibilities for the future. Throughout the process, it is the collaborative, relational aspects that give power to the change effort. Through dialogue and sharing, new realities are born within the organizational system which create the lasting positive change. The foundational principles of the AI methodology are based on social construction theory.

While many AI projects are conducted within the corporate setting, there are numerous applications within schools, churches, non-profit organizations and communities, as well as within private lives. Some AI practitioners, for example, Jane Watkins and Ralph Kelly, hold couples workshops in which they help people to rediscover the glow of love that led them to marriage; the workshop helps to promote loving relationships through explorations of the positives. Others are offering workshops that help people to develop leadership practices and personal lifestyles based on appreciative principles. See the Related Resource section for information on learning opportunities and further readings in AI. The interested reader will find these citations at the end of the book. We now turn to a third context in which constructionist practices are flourishing, education.

Constructionism and the Classroom

As professors of psychology we find that constructionist ideas have powerful effects on our teaching practices. For one, we now try wherever possible to replace lecturing with dialogues with students. Why? Because the traditional conception of teaching is marred by its individualist base and the accompanying failure to acknowledge the relational generation of meaning. Thus, we no longer see it as our duty to "pour knowledge into our students' heads." Rather, we bring to the class what we see as resources that will enable students to engage in new dialogues. However, we also believe that students bring with them useful accounts of the real, the rational and the good. Through dialogue they are able to make use of their skills and to generate meaningful conversation; they must also take into account what others (including we, the teachers) have to say. If the classroom is respectful and accepting, students are animated and engaged. Through dialogue they are most likely to graft onto their personal perspectives what it is we offer from our tradition of knowing. We learn from them as well. Teaching and learning converge.

Of course, we are not alone in our attempts to put constructionist ideas to work in the classroom. Let us explore two active movements favored by constructionist ideas.

Critical Pedagogy and Beyond

Although politicians and school administrators often declare that "good education" is free of political or ideological bias, the constructionist understands that education is inherently political. For example, the simple requirement of proficiency in English declares that all must speak in one language, what many would say is the language of the privileged. The simple removal of religion from the schools declares the society to be fundamentally secular. And more subtly, to favor experimental methods in establishing knowledge of human behavior is to imply that we understand others best when we are dispassionate and manipulative. This is not to argue

that the link between education and value biases is either dangerous or to be avoided. In fact, most of the biases in our curriculum
support the ways of life favored by the majority. (It is only when
they don't support one's way of life that they are likely to be rec-
ognized as biases at all!) If a teacher urges students to vote, that is
not considered a bias, but if she urges them to vote for the Demo-
crats, that is a bias. From a constructionist standpoint, however,
we may also place a value on gaining awareness of these biases,
understanding who is privileged by them and who is rendered in-
visible. In doing so we may begin to envision alternatives. If we
pay attention to which ones speak out in class discussions and which
ones do not, we may learn about silent or missing voices, and how
to empower the silent voices to speak.

Such concerns have long been reflected in the critical pedagogy movement, a movement largely inspired by Paolo Friere's
(1972) book, Pedagogy of the Oppressed. Friere was particularly
concerned with the ways in which many educational systems work
against the lower classes, essentially preparing them for lives of
quiet servitude. Since that time, many other critics have centered
especially on the race and gender biases built into standard cur-
ricula and teaching methods. While it is vital to bring forth the
class, race and gender biases implicit in our traditions of knowledge, constructionism invites further steps. First, there is a need to
expand critical sensitivities so that all people, from all traditions,
may better understand the gaps and silences represented in our
educational practices. Biases are scarcely limited to class, race and
gender. They also function in terms of religion, sexual preference,

traditions of skill (e.g., writing, music, athletics) and much more. It is coming to grips with the multiple realities that forms the greatest educational challenge.

In addition, the constructionist invites us to replace antagonistic critique with dialogue. It is one thing to find one's tradition oppressed, but another to subdue the oppressor. The oppressor also sustains a tradition of value, and, if we set all traditions against each other, life will become nasty, brutish and short. Because there are no ultimate means of judging among traditions, it is important to acquire the arts of mutual exploration. In this context, constructionism asks us to realize the limits of critique. By emphasizing shortcomings, we solidify their reality; we see the negative and little else. There is good reason, then, to supplement practices of critique with explorations of the positive. It is when we also acknowledge what is positive in another's tradition that mutual exploration is most likely to yield new forms of life.

Collaborative Learning

Traditional education is individualist in orientation. It is the mind of the single individual one hopes to improve; the student is judged on the basis of his or her "own work;" and grades are assigned to individuals. However, constructionist ideas raise questions about individualism, both as a view of persons and as a political ideology. Earlier we reasoned that what we call individual "thought" is indeed a byproduct of one's immersion in relationships. Without a language of justice or responsibility, for example, how could we think about such matters? And, as we saw, if we hold the individual as the basic unit of society, we create a culture of separation and alienation. On the other hand, if everything we hold to be real, reasonable and dear is a byproduct of relationship, then it makes sense to place the relational process at the center of the educational practice.

A Dialogue on Personal Practices

Ken: I like these developments in professional practices, but you know, constructionist ideas have also entered our personal lives in important ways. It might be useful for readers to get a feel for constructionist practices in daily relationships.

Mary: Very much on my mind as well. I think about a joke we share about my being irritated with you about being home late for dinner. I ask you accusingly why you are so late, and you respond sweetly with, "What story would you like to hear?" I can't remain in my role of wounded wife; I burst out laughing. I realize that you are reminding me that there are many ways to construct reality, and you are trying to find one that would get us back on a good track.

Ken: Yes, I also remember a time when I returned from work in a rather bad mood. I poisoned the atmosphere when I entered the house. We decided that this was not a good kind of reality in which to live, and you asked that I go outside and enter again. The second time around was much better. We successfully deconstructed the first encounter and made way for a second more constructive one.

Mary: It is really helpful for me to know that if we have created a bad space between us, that it is only one way of being, the result of one way of constructing the world and each other. We can then search for alternatives.

Ken: What is especially wonderful for me is that when I am "down" for any reason, you can show me ways of positively reconstructing the situation. You revive my outlook and energies, and I am enormously grateful.

Mary: I am always searching for ways to feel good about life. This has been especially important to me in times of grave illness. This is also important in the way I relate to others, including kids, colleagues, friends. Bad feelings are the result of bad constructions, and since none of them are True, they can be replaced. The challenge is to find a way to replace them that feels right. I must also say that conversations with others can really be helpful in rearranging the meanings of life.

Increasingly educators are moving in the relational direction. An important outcome of this is collaborative learning, that is, learning with others and through others. The kinds of dialogic practices we discussed earlier are but one example. Perhaps the most celebrated move in the relational direction takes the form of collaborative writing. From elementary school to college, writing teachers are experimenting with moving from individual writing assignments to collaborative writing. In collaborative writing a student is either paired with another writer or placed in a small group. In all cases the students work together to generate a final paper. As teachers find, the collaborative process draws from the strengths or skills of all group members. Some students, for example, may be good at working in abstractions; others may provide wonderful stories that can be used for illustration; still others may have odd or unusual insights; and others may pump enthusiasm into the group. Each can make a unique contribution to the whole. In addition to allowing students to contribute from a position of strength, students also learn from each other. The conceptual student learns from the enthusiastic one, and so on; they all may gain insights from the many voices of appraisal brought to the paper. They are also prepared more adequately to work collaboratively in later life. We turn now to a final site where constructionist practices are especially valuable.

Constructively Confronting Conflict

Conflict is present in the world all over — much of it chilling, some of it devastating. Why is conflict so prevalent, and how can we set out to create more life-sustaining ways of being? These are ancient questions indeed, and so is the history of attempts to reduce conflict. Constructionism offers no strong promises in this regard, but it does provide a point of view and a direction for practices of conflict reduction.

For constructionists, most human conflict can be traced to the processes of meaning making. As people coordinate themselves with each other, so do they come to generate shared languages of the real and the good. These languages are built into their customs and conventions. At the same time, this creation of "us" and "our way" creates an exterior domain of "them" and "their way." Typically people within a tradition come to view the outsiders as misguided, inferior or undesirable. At worst, they are seen as dangerous enemies. Thus, when we share similar views of the real and the good, harmony will prevail. It is when "you see it your way" and "I see it my way," that we face the possibility of "either me or you." As Thomas Cleveland writes in <u>Natural History,</u> "... those who start wars usually seem to believe in the righteousness of their chosen course. It is that capability that makes human beings such a dangerous species."

Approaching conflict from a constructionist standpoint, one avoids the question of who, ultimately, is right or wrong. If we are to move beyond conflict, the central question is how to draw these divergent domains of meaning closer. Because of the centrality of language in constructing these conflicting realities, our attention is particularly drawn to dialogue. Are there ways we might talk with each other that would allow us to live together more amicably?

This emphasis on dialogue is scarcely new, but constructionism asks us to look beyond the conflicting content of our discourses — to consider the forms of talk — how things are said, what is emphasized, where the silences fall and so on. For example, if we disagreed, we could engage in argument. But an argument as a form of dialogue pits us against each other: one side must win, the other loses. Argument is essentially "war by other means." What, then, are some promising alternatives to argument as a way of working things out?

The Public Conversations Project

One very promising practice, developed by a group of family therapists in the Boston area, is called the Public Conversations Project. The group was vitally concerned with the animosity and violence developing around the issue of abortion, both in the Boston area and the country at large. With good people on both sides, intense in their claims of moral right, and both murder and terrorism increasing in frequency, the need for new conversations was pressing. The response of the Public Conversations Project was the creation of a conversational form that did not lead to attack, humiliation and revenge. The process of choosing and gathering people together and helping them converse is elaborately designed. The following is an overview of the process.

On a typical evening, representatives of the adversarial groups are invited to meet together. Rather than placing them into immediate debate, they first have a meal together. Conversations on the issues that separate them are not allowed; in fact, at this stage there is no way for participants to identify each other's position on the issues. Thus, the meal proceeds with talk about mutual interests — work, children, the weather and the like. A sense of sharing in a common humanity typically prevails. When the discussion program begins, the facilitators insist that the participants talk on a personal, experiential level rather than exchanging principles well known to each side of the discussion. Participants are especially encouraged to tell personal stories related to their positions. They often speak of pain or suffering they had experienced around the issue. While participants might resist an argument based on principles, they can listen sympathetically to these stories. As a result they begin to understand emotionally why those on the other side feel as they do. Later, participants are also encouraged to speak of their "gray areas," that is, of their doubts in the positions they hold. Here they begin to reveal a second voice, one that begins to resemble that of the opposition.

One outcome of this carefully orchestrated conversation among 6-10 participants is usually a de-escalation of the conflict. Participants are not asked to change their positions (nor do they), but they are able to gain a more sympathetic understanding of the other side. Further, at times they begin to construct new possibilities. For example, in the case of pro-life vs. pro-choice, participants could agree to work together to prevent situations in which abortion might become an option. In one case, they agreed to warn the others in times of impending danger. Some participants have been so drawn to these conversations that they have met privately to continue their talks over a number of years. In effect, through fashioning a form of conversation, mutual hatred gave way to collaborative inquiry. As a constructionist approach to conflict resolution there is an understanding that neither side has the truth or that there are many sides to an issue. Dialogue together can creatively construct new outcomes.

Summary Focus

Practices in therapy, organizational change, education and community conflict reduction have all been stimulated by constructionist ideas. We have highlighted the therapeutic practices of narrative therapy, brief and solution-focused therapies, and postmodern therapy. In organizational change practices we have looked at relational leadership and Appreciative Inquiry. Among educational practices we took note of critical pedagogy and collaborative learning approaches. Through dialogue and particularly the Public Conversation Project, ways of reducing conflict were shown. In another volume we could also write about new practices in counseling, social work, religion and more. Our special hope is that the reader may also be stimulated by our discussion to locate other arenas in which these ideas may inspire innovation. It is from relationship that the future is molded.

Chapter 4

Research as
Construction Practice

Many of our traditional assumptions about knowledge and the practice of research are challenged by constructionist ideas. In the present chapter we first describe some of the major shifts in understanding invited by constructionism. We then turn to some applications of these ideas in social science research. If constructionism offers an alternative view of knowledge, what does this mean for the ways we seek knowledge of each other and ourselves?

Reconstructing Knowledge Practices

Traditionally the search for knowledge has been closely associated with the search for Truth. In contrast to this tradition, constructionists understand knowledge as the product of particular communities, guided by particular assumptions, beliefs and values. There is no "Truth for all," but instead "truth within community." People who are called "ignorant" are not lacking all knowledge; they simply are not part of the community that may view them as such. They function with knowledge of a different kind. For example, mathematics professors do not know more than basketball players or historians more than bricklayers. Each group's knowledge functions in a different way for different purposes. This shift toward pluralities of knowledge sets the stage for further constructionist challenges to our traditions of making knowledge.

Disturbing Disciplinary Boundaries

Disciplines of scientific knowledge, such as chemistry or geology, are largely based on the idea that there is *objective* truth about the world, which can be discovered. In this tradition, each discipline has special *objects of study* (e.g., chemical elements, animal species, the economy, the mind) and each requires specialized research methods (e.g., experiments, laboratory apparatus, sample analysis). This orientation has led to the development of isolated islands of knowledge makers who infrequently communicate with each other and who are rarely intelligible to the public at large. On most university campuses, each department of knowledge is typically housed in a different building; inhabitants rarely visit their neighbors. Those in the "ivory tower" are even less inclined to communicate with the public outside.

Constructionism poses a challenge to such isolation. For the constructionist, the objects of research are constructed by the relevant communities of knowledge makers. Communities create the reality of chemistry, economics, psychology, physics and so on. As the famous historian of science, Thomas Kuhn, proposed, communities develop *paradigms*; a paradigm is constituted by the shared set of assumptions, methods, ways of writing, rewards and so on that hold the community together. Paradigms are the "engines" of sense making in a community. Within these paradigms, problems valued by the community are solved. While there are important gains to be made within these paradigms, there are also limitations. The paradigm often functions like a blinder. Once you are inside, it is difficult to see beyond. If your reality is "material," for example, anyone who mentions "spirit" will appear to be talking about nothing at all. If your paradigm challenges you to split an atom, which might be useful for a bomb, questions about the good and evil of warfare are largely irrelevant. Those questions are in the realm of politics or religion, not of science as such.

The constructionist challenge, then, is to blur the disciplinary boundaries. Our ultimate welfare lies in cross-talk, the kind of dialogue that allows multiple realities and values to intersect. The failure to share brings about blindness to the values and potentials of alternative traditions. It is also essential to bring disciplines of scholarship into dialogue with the surrounding culture. Through these encounters, all parties are enriched; most important, scholarly and scientific work is more likely to speak to issues of general significance to society. This point is closely associated with a second argument.

Inquiring into Utility and Value

As constructionists see it, research within a paradigm may be highly valued by the community committed to this paradigm. Economists may appreciate the fruits of economic modeling, and neuroscientists may take great interest in the results of neuro-image research. However, the constructionist also asks us to consider the utility of such languages and their outcomes *outside the bounds* of the community. How does economic research or neuro-imaging, for example, contribute to (or possibly undermine) the lives of those in the society more generally? Do those outside the disciplines have a voice in making such judgments?

These are essentially questions of value. What ways of life do we wish to encourage? What do we wish for our children and grandchildren? For example, historians are charged with telling us the truth about history. But how should the history of the Middle East be described? Much depends on who is telling the story, in what era, and for what purpose. Some accounts will favor the Islamic religion; others will not. Some accounts will say that many Islamic countries have failed to enter the modern era of technology; while others will say that they have succeeded in resisting the deterioration of their tradition. There is no stepping out of all traditions to write this history. And as long as we are embroiled in such conflicts of viewpoints, dialogue on these matters is essential. If all else fails, the alternative can be mutual annihilation.

Encouraging Multiple Methods

Traditional research assumes that there is a world of objects or events separate from the researcher. It is the job of the researcher to reveal their character. Typically this means locating a sensitive and accurate measure of the subject matter. For example, those who believe that "attitudes" exist in people's minds develop survey questions to "tap people's attitudes." Those who believe in "economic process," might use the GNP (Gross National Product) as a measure of economic progress. In effect, there is a prevailing belief that one can find "truth through method."

From a constructionist perspective, research methods reflect the assumptions and values of a particular community. Thus, methods do not give us reflections of nature so much as create what we take to be nature. If psychologists value something called "intelligence" and they are willing to define certain actions (such as solving verbal problems) as intelligent, then they can develop a measure of intelligence called IQ. But people's responses to an intelligence test are only indicators of intelligence according to the way psychologists define the world. Intelligence tests do not then reflect "differences in intelligence." Rather they construct a world in which such differences in intelligence seem obvious. The same is the case for measures of self-esteem, personality, cognitive functioning and so on.

We are not suggesting that we abandon traditional research methods despite this view of the power of methods to create reality. Recall that all truth is "within a tradition" and that each tradition sustains certain values. Thus, for particular purposes the research methods of a tradition can make a valuable contribution. If we construct the world in terms of physical health and illness, and wish to avoid the latter, then methods of medical research are invaluable. This does not make medical science True, or its methods superior for all. One must agree with the tradition and its values. Often there is little opportunity for questioning these values. For example, discussions of the best method for testing intelligence are common. However, seldom is attention given to the question of whether or not we should honor the notion of "intelligence." The concept is highly valuative in nature; it credits certain people at the expense of others. Yet we do not ask what kind of society we create when we place all its members on such a scale and pronounce that approximately half are below average.

Expanding Forms of Expression

Most scientific research is communicated to peers through written reports. For those outside the community, such reports are often difficult to read and even those within communities often find them overly complex and boring. Such writing styles can be traced in part to a "tradition of Truth" that emphasizes precise statements of hard facts and abhors rhetorical styles that might bias the reader. As it is said, scientists must keep passion outside the framework of their writing so that it does not cloud the reader's judgments. However, if we understand truth as a communal creation, these demands on writing are no longer binding. Rather, we are challenged to view scientific writing as a way of relating within a community.

In this light, we can understand traditional scientific writing as but one possible form of expression, useful for certain purposes (e.g., efficiency of communication among an elite group of scientists) but limited in other respects. For example, if scientific writing speaks only to scientists, then those outside the science cannot enter the dialogue. The sciences become exclusionary. In social science, where common citizens are often the subjects of research, this criticism is especially important. Social science has a long history of finding fault with various groups of people, effectively calling them "unintelligent," "narrow minded," "conforming," "mentally deficient," "prejudiced," and the like. However, these forms of writing give little room for the "victims" either to understand or respond to these descriptions.

Informed by such arguments, many scholars, particularly in the social sciences, experiment with new forms of writing. Through new forms, new realities are constructed. Some use their "personal voice" to present their research. By writing in the first person about one's experiences, the account is more appealing to read and it reveals the flesh and blood engagement of the scientist. Such writing also implies that the account is a construction and that others might see it differently. Other writers experiment with multiple voices to reveal different perspectives. In a recent dissertation written by a Maori counseling psychologist in New Zealand, three different voices (and type fonts) were included in the text. Her scholarly voice (dispassionate and objective), her personal voice (strongly passionate), and a Maori voice (written in the language of her own people).

In one fascinating case, Karen Fox features the voice of a therapy client who has been sexually abused by her stepfather. However, she also interviews the stepfather, who is in prison for sexual abuse. Finally, because she herself had been a victim of sexual abuse, she includes her own voice. Each of the three voices is streamed simultaneously on the page, so that one not only experiences the multiple perspectives but also gains further by understanding through their juxtaposition. Here is a small excerpt:

Ben: Sex Offender

When they first came to live with me ... They never had much before. They were eating pancakes most of the time ... I took them to places. Their father never did that. So I was around more.

Sherry: Victim

He gave us a life we didn't have. I didn't eat meat until I was 7. We lived on pancakes and eggs. He gave us a home. He gave us discipline. We kids were out of control.... There is no way, shape, and form that the good he did out-weighed the bad. This doesn't excuse what he did. I've had feelings of love for him, like a father.

Karen: the Researcher

Betty Ann, his wife, says Ben and Sherry were very close. They talked about everything together. She talked with him about her period....

Ben: Sex Offender

As long as we sex offenders are in denial, we can't get help. We have to admit to what we did. What I did was wrong. I know that now.

Sherry: Victim

I think it is sinking in. He's getting help. Nobody gets well in two years.

Yet, one might be even more daring and ask, why the emphasis on writing in the presentation of research? There are many forms of representation available to us, and words are so restricting. Why not use film, audio recordings, music, art, dance, multi-media and more? Each form of representation offers new possibilities for constructing the world and for relating both within and outside the knowledge making communities. Such challenges are as exciting as they are radical in their implications. There is, however, ample precedent for such work. Anthropologists have used film to document the lives of tribal peoples for nearly a century. These visual recordings are often more informative than the verbal reports. With the use of recording devices, everyone is furnished with the potential to share otherwise undocumented ways of life. New constructions of the world can be produced through new forms of media. Each one has a different capacity to create reality.

Social Change Through Photographs

For many years social researcher, M. Brinton Lykes, has been working with women in the mountainous regions of Guatemala. These women suffered greatly as a result of civil wars raging over their lands; family members were killed and villages were destroyed by enemy troops. As part of a research endeavor and a mode of healing and solidarity building among the women, Lykes gave each of them a camera. In this way they could document the destruction and violence that had taken place. She then arranged for the women to share the photographs with each other and to talk about the implications of these scenes for their lives. Conversations about the photographs lead to a deeper, more complex understanding of events, and they also helped pave the way for rebuilding community. Using the photographs, the women were given the unusual opportunity to express their visions of life and the future. Through the sharing they developed the kind of solidarity and inspiration to bring about change. Their photographs and dialogues helped them to create new realities, ones that allowed them new visions and plans for the future. For these women, a greater hopefulness about who they were and what they might become resulted from this socially constructed endeavor.

The Flowering of Social Research Methods

These four challenges — breaking disciplinary boundaries, evaluating societal functions, encouraging multiple methods and expanding forms of expression are relevant to all sectors of knowledge making. As you might imagine, however, constructionist ideas have had more impact within the social sciences and humanities than the natural sciences. In these former areas, a burgeoning of new research practices has occurred. Here we illustrate a number of these developments. Specifically we explore unfolding explorations in narrative study, discourse analysis, ethnography and action research.

Narrating the Self

In traditional research, the social scientist observes and draws conclusions about others, their motives, problems, habits, relationships and so on. The constructionist asks, however, "Why don't we allow people the right to speak in their own voice? Did our subjects authorize us to speak for them? Do we even know if they would agree with our conclusions?" Rather than writing *about them*, why not let them portray their lives?

One significant means for giving research subjects voice is through narrative methods. You may recall our discussion of narratives in previous chapters. In the present case researchers enable people to tell their own stories. They may, for example, collect life stories, analyze autobiographies or locate letters in historical archives. Thus, narrative research has been used to provide insight into aging, immigrating, becoming a criminal, taking drugs, "coming out" and much more. These stories are important not only in giving us a sense of the realities in which other people live, but in enabling us to see life from their point of view.

Wrestling with the Monomyth of Achievement

To illustrate the narrative approach at work, consider Mary Gergen's research on the autobiographies of high achieving Americans. As the autobiographies of leaders in business, science, the arts and sports suggested to her, men's lives seem dominated by what is often called the monomyth, that is the ancient myth of a man who goes on a quest, (e.g., to slay the dragon, defeat a foe), and then emerges as an enlightened and victorious hero. This myth, it seems, functions as a resource for men; it provides a template to guide their lives. At the same time, when she examined the autobiographies of high achieving women, she found little evidence of the monomyth. Rather, women achievers seem to be poor storytellers; they often describe relationships that are important to them, but unrelated to their career pursuits. Gergen wondered if the absence of a monomyth in women's lives was one reason they were less likely to be high achievers? Or perhaps more importantly, was it possible that the common narrative form was too narrow to encompass the activities of contemporary women? And in a world where relationships are central to all that takes place, is the monomyth a promising form of narrative to guide young lives, or is it a straight jacket? This too, is a question of value, and men and women often take different views of it.

Studies in Discourse

The highly influential French theorist, Michel Foucault, illuminated the way in which various communities — in science, religion, government and the like — produce *disciplinary regimes*. A disciplinary regime is a set of rules we learn that regulate our conduct and our expressions. When we absorb a discipline we learn to behave in certain ways and not in others. Rather than having others watching over our every move, we learn to police ourselves so that we do not do things that might be regarded as stupid, disgusting or evil. Yet, disciplines also create a blindness to that which is outside; they close down possibilities, and lead to a disparaging of those outside the discipline. Influenced by such arguments, many constructionist scholars are drawn to the study of discourse and its impact on society.

Researchers are particularly concerned with how the ways we talk and write shape our patterns of life. How are the words we use inviting us in one direction and blinding us to others? Discourse analysts wish to illuminate the languages by which we live, not simply because the languages are interesting, but because they wish to stimulate social change. They want to challenge our common sense, our taken for granted worlds, in order that we can be free to do otherwise. For example, by drawing attention to the taken for granted distinction between heterosexual and homosexual — straight and gay — we begin to see that our categories are limited. We divide our complex world of sexual relationship into two exclusive categories, even when we realize that people's sexual lives are often much more complex. By examining the common discourse more carefully and more critically, we are invited to reconsider our ways of life and to search for new paths. In the case of sexuality we may begin to develop new terms — polysexual, LUG (lesbian until graduation), bisexuality, etc. — that invite new patterns of cultural life. As many see it, the focus of discourse research is liberation.

"I'm too old to do that ..." A Killer Explanation

The state of Illinois suffered a shortage of nurses. Sociologist, Chris Bodily, set out to study why nurses who were over 50 years of age were not working nor did they seem interested in returning to the field. Scanning over 1,000 survey responses, he was struck with the number of times the respondents used age as their explanation for retirement. Comments such as "because of my age ..." or "It would be impossible at my age ..." were used as if it were just obvious that they could not continue working. Yet, as Bodily points out, there is nothing about the number of years one has lived that precludes continued productivity. Using a similar discourse, people say, "I am too old for jogging," "playing tennis," or "having a love affair." However, research suggests that declines in physical fitness are primarily the result of decreased physical activity rather than the opposite. In effect, our physical potential does not decline dramatically because we grow older; rather, we decline physically with age largely because we cease being active. By maintaining activity levels, older people can lower their blood pressure, reduce anxiety, improve sleep patterns, strengthen bones, improve cardiovascular endurance and in virtually every aspect become healthier and stronger. Unless they accept the common discourse, "I am too old ..." possibly an invitation to a premature death.

Lived Worlds: Ethnographic Adventures

The aim of much traditional research is to establish a set of abstract theories or principles, with the hope of predicting human behavior. For many constructionists, abstract theories seem cut away from daily life and insensitive to change across time. Further, one never knows when, where and how an abstract concept applies to a

84

particular situation. As a result many social researchers have abandoned the quest for abstract theory in favor of ethnographic research, — studies illuminating the lives of various groups of peoples. As it is reasoned, in gaining an understanding of how other people live and construct their worlds, we broaden our own horizons, our appreciations and potentials for living. The result has been a flowering of ethnographic methods.

To be sure, ethnographic study is scarcely new within the social sciences. Initially such inquiry developed in anthropology. Here researchers would typically travel to distant lands and live with tribal communities. They studied the Trobriand islanders, the Balinese, the Minangkabau, and so on. With the disappearance of "exotic" cultures untouched by western ways, there was a turn to the various sub-cultures within modern societies. Here sociologists often joined with anthropologists to study small ethnic communities, religious cults, sex workers, body builders and motorcycle gangs, all groups that were relatively inaccessible to the culture at large.

Ethnographic study appeals to many constructionists, not only because it illuminates alternative constructions of the world, but also because it doesn't require the kind of manipulation and deceit often accompanying laboratory experiments. However, constructionist ideas are also opening up new vistas in ethnography. Here are two of the more exciting developments:

- *Collaborative ethnography.* Researchers increasingly ask, "What gives me the right to report on others, to translate their lives into my words; why shouldn't people have the right to define for others who they are?" Such reflection has stimulated many researchers to seek out ways of working collaboratively with people they wish to study. For example, several years ago, James Scheurich, a colleague in Texas, was interested in giving expression to the experience of immigrant Mexicans in the state. He gained the cooperation of two graduate students with Mexican backgrounds, and they set about creating a research "happening" or performance to which people were invited. There were many visual, aesthetic and intellectual offerings available to those who participated. Various immigrants shared their stories in writing, on tape recordings, and in photographs and slides. Along with music and poetry, there were presentations that included audience participation. The effect was to present the experience as polyvocal, without a core theme or a dominant metaphor. There was no one Mexican immigrant experience. Visitors were able to resonate in their own particular way with the events. Such an approach, which emphasized the constructive potential of each viewer/ participant, avoided the threat of rejection or of denial that a single voiced presentation might evoke. Through their presentation they emphasized that there is no simple or singular understanding of others' lives.

• *Autoethnography*. Researchers increasingly ask, "Why should I report on the lives of others when I have never lived in their shoes?" This kind of reflection has stimulated the development of autoethnography — the revealing of one's own life experiences to illuminate a given sub-culture. For example, Carol

86

Rambo Ronai has written about her employment as a "pole dancer" and mud-wrestler at a "Gentleman's Club." Her autoethnography is both reflexive and descriptive of the sense of herself, the relational ties among the girls, the boss and the audience and the atmosphere of the club that surrounds this type of business. Her account is full of drama, emotional tension, violence, and sensual excitement and revulsion. Her goal, as a dancer and as a scholar, is to let the reader know more about the experiences of being a dancer in such a club than a less emotional, more uninvolved, portrayal could give:

"As Kitty steps out of the ring, the declared winner, I smack her derriere. She looks back at me, tired, and ignores me. I hit her rear again with everything I've got. The sound of the smack reverberates through the room. The crowd ignites ... Kitty rushes and dives on top of me. The crowd loves it. To emphasize the point that she has just won, she sits on my chest with her arms raised in a gesture of triumph. Drained, exhausted, and humiliated ... I go to the dressing room to change my clothes.... My emotions are a collage of calm meditative moments punctuated by outbursts where I want to cry.... Reality vibrates with the hum of the machinery in the building. It threatens to close in on me. I desperately look for something else to attend to, choking back fright with a contrived calm." (Pg. 119-120)

Making New Worlds: Action Research

One of the most dramatic differences between research favored by traditionalists and constructionists lies in their contrasting views of personal and social change. Traditional research tends to presume a high degree of stability in human conduct. For example, researchers focus on processes of cognition, leadership, ethnic differences or social structure as if they are all relatively enduring. Relying especially on neurological and evolutionary theories, psychologists often presume that today's research findings are relevant to all times and all cultures. In contrast, constructionists emphasize the potential for human change; because they see forms of cultural life held together by shared meaning and values, with transformations in discourse and values, cultural life may dramatically change. The rapid rise of Maoism in China, the deterioration of the Soviet Union, the collapse of Apartheid in South Africa, and the rise of global terrorism are only a few examples. Whether yesterday's research will be useful tomorrow is always an open question.

In this light, researchers are increasingly drawn to the possibilities of using research not for purposes of charting the past in order to predict the future, but creating new futures directly. Dedicated to this end is action research. Originating in the 1970's, action research shared much of the intellectual and political fervor of the times. These researchers did not remain tucked in their laboratory, studying people and animals for the sake of publishing journal articles for their peers and for long-term scientific payoffs. Rather, they went out and offered their services to those in need. In particular, they hoped that such research could help liberate people from oppressive political and economic conditions and generate new possibilities of life for them. This special form of research commitment has grown over the years, especially in Britain, Scandinavia, and in South America. By the late 1990's a World Symposium of Action Research held in Cartagena, Colombia, brought together 2,000 delegates from 61 countries. At the present time, the major goals of action research include the alleviation of suffering, the establishment of justice, the reduction of conflict and the enhancement of democratic process. Action research is utilized is various practices including organization development, education, community development and therapy.

Action Research in Action

A youth drop-in center for street kids in Ottawa, Canada, was facing a crisis. Some thought the center needed more structure and rules; others thought there should be more counselors and staff; still others thought the center should be closed in order to discourage the young "riff raff" from hanging around the neighborhood. The center was supported by the city youth service agency, which decided to study the center and then reform it. However, rather than using the traditional method of studying from a distance and announcing the results, the chosen method of study was action research. Specifically, the researchers developed a partnership with the youth, hoping they could join in actively creating their own futures within the center. Researchers and the youth center facilitators assisted them in the process. The research team consisted of 6 youths, 2 center facilitators and an outside researcher.

The first step in this action research, the team building process, required that the youth come to know and trust the process and the adults involved. The goal of the group was to assess the center, make recommendations to the agency and help the center serve its constituents better. The group reached these ends through an 18 month long set of struggles and triumphs. By coming into ownership of the process, the street kids engaged fully and were able to assess the center in vitally important ways. They engaged in creative activities with their adult compatriots, including building a "kit," which was the basis of their presentations to outside groups and to other kids. While the content of the kit was based on solid data, its presentation was boisterous, colorful and full of life and humor. Through these joint endeavors, the center became a vibrant element in the lives of the youth and contributed significantly to the future of the facility, which was assured through their efforts.

Summary Focus

As constructionist ideas enter communities of research, self-reflection, enthusiasm and innovation occur. The social sciences are currently in a state of major transformation and the future is scarcely fixed. Constructionist ideas favor pluralism — multiple voices, methods and values. Among the research forms described here were narrative study, discourse analysis, ethnography, and action research. Each of these emphasizes a constructionist approach to broadening understanding of social realities and helping change take place within involved communities. Yet, with such free-flowing pluralism we also set the stage for creative collusions and collisions. If we are fortunate transformation will continue.

Chapter 5

From Critique to
Collaboration

For many people constructionist ideas are deeply unsettling. They call into question the realities and values central to daily life without providing a clear slate of alternatives. Because they undermine foundational claims to truth, objectivity and moral certitude, they have played a central role in what are called the "culture wars." Here critics resist the possibility that every sub-culture has a right to its own truths and values. Constructionist ideas have also contributed centrally to the "science wars" in which critics resist the possibility that scientific truth is only one truth among many. As you can thus appreciate, constructionism has come under severe attack from many quarters.

In the present chapter, we take up some of the central lines of critique. To be sure we will try to provide compelling counters to these critiques. However, it is important to note the form of our answers as well as the content. If we were committed to only a single truth, form of reason or set of values we might try to demonstrate that the critic was simply wrong — guilty, let us say, of making some fundamental error. However, from a constructionist standpoint there are no fundamental errors. We need not fight to the end to ensure that constructionist views prevail over all others. Rather, we can use the critique as an invitation to dialogue and possible collaborations out of which might emerge new understandings, insights or departures. We search, then, for answers that do not accuse and alienate the critic, but those which might draw us together in creating the "new." Three common critiques will concern us here, the critique of nihilism, realism and moral relativism.

From Nihilism to Enriched Realities

Many people are alarmed at the ways in which constructionist ideas seem to undermine all beliefs. According to constructionism, they complain, we can't trust science to tell us the truth; it is only a story. Likewise, everything we presume about history, politics, world conditions, religion and so on are only stories. Doesn't this just leave us in a nihilistic void? Is nothing true; is there nothing on which we can rely or in which we can believe? And, if everything we hold as true and good is a construction, aren't we moved to apathy; aren't we relieved of having to ask the hard questions about the future, or even worse, of having to act at all?

To respond to this charge, constructionists do have sympathy with the desire for reliable realities. And, who would not wish to identify when an account is true as opposed to false? Don't we all want to hold fast to the fact that "this medicine will cure your infection," and "this plane flies to San Francisco?" We want to be sure that news reporters and scientists do not falsify their reports. In this sense, constructionists are scarcely nihilists. There is room here for collaborative creation.

In this spirit, let us first consider the implications of lamenting, "It is only a social construction." This phrase is significant

92

chiefly because we cling to the view that some accounts of reality are not social constructions, that some "get it right" about the world. If we abandon the view that some particular arrangement of words is uniquely tailored to the world as it is, then we are freed from the curse of nihilism. That is, constructionism doesn't mean giving up something called truth; rather we are simply invited to see truth claims of all kinds as born out of relationships in particular cultural and historical conditions. This does not make the claims of medicine, news reporters or air pilots untrue or unreliable. Rather, we come to realize that all such claims are very useful within particular circumstances. If we agree in our constructions of disease, life and death, we will want to rely on medical claims of cure; if we concur on the meaning of "flying to San Francisco," we will count on the pilot's telling us the truth about our destination. Within a tradition, truth claims are essential to successful functioning.

With the importance of local truths established, we are prepared for two additional moves of significance. First, there is reason to resist the attempt of any particular group to claim that its local truths are universal or that they should replace all others. Human history bears enormous scars resulting from the attempts of one group to force their truth — about god, justice, the master race or the nature of evil — onto others. The point is especially important in current world conditions where various cultural beliefs are thrown into increasing conflict, and where there is a strong tendency in Western culture to believe its truths are superior to others. If we are to live together peacefully on the planet, it is important that no particular group feels justified to obliterate all dissenting realities.

Of equal significance, by emphasizing the advantages of local truth, we also invite an exploration of alternatives to our comfortable visions of the true and the good. It is not simply that we are cautioned against over-stepping the boundaries of our local realities. We are also encouraged to seek out alternative constructions, with the realization that these constructions are highly functional to those who developed them. In this sense a scientist need not turn a blind eye to spiritualism — or even creationism. These latter truths are not contenders for scientific status; rather, these discourses serve other functions. They give the kind of value and meaning to the universe that science cannot provide. And, rather than condemning out of hand those who participate in so-call "terrorist" activities, it may be useful to enter into their world of meaning and to understand how their actions are justified within their communities. With full, mutual exchange, we may find means of co-creating alternatives to mutual annihilation.

Beyond Realism: Bodies, Mind and Power

Closely related to critiques of nihilism are those that argue that constructionist ideas do not square with the obvious facts of life. Resistance is particularly strong in three quarters. First, there are critics who consider the human body as central to an understanding of social life. For them the body is an inescapable reality. As often proposed, our bodies define us; we experience the world through our bodies; and as the body changes so does our sense of the world and self. Second, there are critics who hold the private world of the mind as central. Don't we use our minds to interpret the character of our experience of the world and don't our emotions and thoughts influence what we do? Finally, many social scientists are critical of the constructionist failure to deal with the obvious differences in power between various social groups. If we don't confront differences in power, they say we cannot relieve the oppressive conditions under which so many people live. If we don't make power central to our analysis, we are implicitly supporting the status quo. If, for example, poverty, oppression, starvation and genocide are only constructions, then we are unmotivated to act.

These critiques are often labeled *realist*, in that they wish to hold firm to certain specific reality claims; they are also called *essentialist*, in that they declare something — body, mind or power in this case — as an essential or undeniable aspect of the world that precedes language. They are important criticisms. Who would wish, after all, to abandon concern with the body, the mind or the structures of domination and injustice in society? But, before we consider ways of collaborating with these concerns, it is important to point out a fundamental misunderstanding that often accompanies these critiques. Constructionist ideas primarily function at what might be called a *meta-level*. That is, they try to account for how it is we come to share our common conceptions of the real and the good. They try to explain, for example, how we come to understand our bodies as "machines," as opposed to "holy vessels." They are concerned with the Western conception of the mind and ways in which it differs from other cultures; they point to the many ways in which power is constructed, and the advantages and disadvantages attached to each. In effect, *constructionists try to understand our understandings*, and in doing so, offer a set of tools or discourses that can be used for many purposes. You may recall here the metaphor of constructionism as a broad umbrella under which all forms of reality-making can be considered — even the seeming reality created by constructionism itself.

Unfortunately, critics often mistake this meta-level account as the constructionist attempt to tell the real truth about the world. As they see it, if we leave out the body, the mind or power from this account we are blind. But this is to misunderstand the attempt. At this level the hope is simply to generate a consciousness of possibility, an orientation to meaning and to knowledge, and not "the new truth." Rather, under the constructionist umbrella we will surely want to consider these realities; at the meta-level they are not required. In this context, let us move under the umbrella to work collaboratively with the proponents of body, mind and power. In this case there are three major options for working creatively together.

1) Join the reality making.

Constructionist meta-theory does not demand any one way of understanding the world, and thus, one is free to explore the potentials of any existing vision. To be sure, most all of us treat the body and mind as parts of everyday reality, and there is no requirement for the constructionist (or anyone else) to discontinue these practices. Although we are deeply engaged with constructionist ideas, the two of us readily participate in everyday talk about bodies and emotion. Such terms are enormously important to our being able to exist effectively in our relationships. Readily we join the reality making.

At the same time, this does not mean casting aside constructionist ideas. Engaging in local realities does not mean abandoning constructionism any more than appreciation of Mozart means abandoning one's love of the blues. And too, constructionist ideas can be extremely useful to us when we talk about bodies, minds and power. For example, many scholars are concerned with oppression and injustice, and committed to changing what they see as the power structure. These same scholars turn to constructionist arguments to undermine the realities served up by government officials. They show how an official declaration of fact is an ideological construction, and should be challenged. Aren't we the richer for being able to use all the discourses, constructionist and realist alike? In order to join in everyday conversations, it is vital to participate in "reality" talk with others.

2) Explore limits together.

Although everyday talk is typically realist (real for us at the moment), constructionism also invites us to consider together the limits of our language. For example, the discourse of power is enormously important in motivating our struggle for justice. In the Western tradition, we can scarcely tolerate the idea that other people control our actions and are living well at the cost of our servitude. However, this vision of power is also divisive. It creates others ("the powerful") as villains; it invites an aggressive posture in which the villains must be vanquished. It is we who now acquire the power!

Of course, when those we single out as "the powerful villains" hear of our discontent, they are thrown into a defensive posture. They feel they have good reasons for what they do and assume we aim to destroy them and the good they have created. Soon we occupy armed and separate camps. The possibilities of working collaboratively toward a just society are minimal. Mutual elimination is favored. Thus, while we join in forms of everyday talk, we try to be aware of their limitations.

3) Create new visions together.

The exploration of limits leads naturally to a final option, which is to work together in creating new and possibly more viable forms of understanding and action. Consider again the concept of power. Rather than viewing power as a structure, with bad people at the top and the good at the bottom, we might think of power as emerging from ongoing relations. If enough people begin to share the same views and values, they will tend to organize themselves, to develop a sense of themselves as united, to generate agendas and plans, and ultimately to become effective in achieving their ends. In brief, they will create a center of power. On this view, there may be multiple centers of power in a culture and these may rapidly change as conversations move on. When we view power as distributed in this way, social change means working together with many different groups. These groups could indeed include many of those who might otherwise appear as enemies at the top. Imagine an organization creating a forum for every person, layer, level, etc. to dialogue about hopes and dreams for the organization. Imagine a community or city creating a dialogue inviting every citizen, young and old, rich and poor, into a conversation about hopes and dreams for the future. Constructionism does not abandon traditions of meaning, but invites moves toward more viable mutuality.

Beyond Moral Relativism

A final and frequent critique of social constructionism points to what seems a moral flabbiness. As it is proposed, constructionism seems to destroy the foundations of all moral visions, while failing to replace them with ideals of its own. Constructionists often propose that all bases for ethical standards or religious principles are generated within particular communities. In this sense, such standards and principles are not divinely given, rationally necessitated or universally binding. As critics bemoan, all morals thus seem to be equal; constructionists can't say that kindness is better than cruelty, diplomacy preferable to genocide and so on. We might be left then with a "whatever" attitude.

To be sure, who would be content to see all standards of the good destroyed? And don't we all prefer certain ways of life to others? Do any of us wish to see human brutality as equal to any other way of treating people? Constructionists are no less participants in society than anyone else and, in this respect, have deep investments in various visions of the good. Constructionism does not invite one to escape all moral visions; to do so would be to step out of all tradition. Rather, it invites us to appreciate our local visions and to be watchful of those who would destroy them. Indeed,

99

for many scholars it is precisely the understanding of moral ideologies as human constructions that have enabled them to speak out. For feminists, racial minority activists, gay rights activists, ex-mental patient groups, the deaf culture and other minorities constructionist ideas have been deeply empowering. They invite open questioning of the status quo and the legitimating of one's otherwise marginalized standpoint.

Given that both constructionists and their critics are invested in some form of moral life, the challenge is to locate common ground for building a viable future. This dialogue might usefully begin with the following question: Would we wish to grant any group the right to declare their moral system universal and to force it onto the remainder of the world? Given the many moral orientations making up the world, we would probably answer "no," for it is quite clear that cultures are in striking disagreement about the precise nature of the good. Whether children of 8 should work in a rug factory to help support their families is open to multiple arguments on both sides; whether Israel should withdraw from the former Palestinian lands or build a wall to keep out Palestinians produces moral controversies on all sides. Should the US president have the power to alter the Geneva Conventions to protect prisoners from torture when there is a terrorist threat is highly contentious. Whose traditions should we destroy; whose tyranny should we accept?

In this sense, our problems do not lie in people's lack of moral values; we are all embedded within traditions that value certain actions while condemning others. The major challenge lies in the abundance of moral goods and the tenacity with which we hold them. At this point constructionist ideas begin to make an important contribution. If all moral goods are born within traditions of relationship, we must first recognize the virtual inevitability of difference, not only lodged within our traditions, but also newly developing every day. Further, because moral values are cultural constructions, we do not have to do battle over which is the superior or the best system. The search for the superior moral code is no more fruitful than locating the superior genre of music or cuisine as preparation for eliminating all the others. Rather, for the constructionist, the challenge is primarily pragmatic. If we do not wish for people to force their visions of the good on others or to see conflicts end in genocide, we must launch a new inquiry together. We must join together to consider practical means of dealing with value conflicts. We must locate or create effective practices for softening the edges of difference, crossing borders and forming new relationships.

Here again, constructionists can make an important contribution. As we have seen in previous chapters, constructionist ideas have encouraged a variety of practices for enhancing coordination among people, for bringing diverse people into a common cause and for reducing differences among antagonists. In a broad sense, all such practices enable people to move beyond a single moral commitment — the one True belief — and to live together with multiplicity. In their best sense, they move us beyond mere tolerance to an appreciation of a pluralistic world. This does not mean a sluggish relativism. Rather, with deep mutuality we will all be transformed and these transformations will leave us with new forms of life in which we can live more easily together. At present we are only beginning to develop the necessary forms of practice. The future is now in our hands.

Summary Focus

In this chapter we raised the critiques of nihilism, realism and moral relativism and attempted to answer each of them. If there is one over-arching problem with most existing critiques of social construction, it is their lodgment in an outmoded view of Truth. By and large, critics approach constructionist ideas as if they are candidates for universal truth. Critics of constructionism believe that, to accept constructionism as True means that all other knowledge claims (typically their own) must be flawed or false. Yet, as we have tried to demonstrate, constructionist ideas challenge the assumption that there is one transcendent truth. For constructionists, *language is used by people to do things together*. The richer our discourses, the greater our capacities for human coordination. This is not to declare that constructionist ideas are True. Rather, constructionism invites new forms of understanding and action. The important issue concerns its implications for our future. In our view, it is a wonderfully useful discourse for it supplies a unique invitation to multiplicity and innovation. It provides hope for an unfolding dialogue among all, for the continuous integration and invention of life forms, and the replacement of lethal conflict with life-giving communion. We hope that in the course of this book, our readers will also have come to appreciate these potentials.

Related Resources

Chapter 1: The Drama of Social Construction

Berger, Peter & Luckmann, Thomas, (1966). The <u>Social Construction of Reality</u>. New York: Doubleday. (The first book in the social sciences that articulated the notion of social constructionism. However, their emphasis was placed on social structures and cognitive processes in the process of generating meaning as opposed to our emphasis on people in relationship.)

Gergen, Kenneth J. (1999). <u>An Invitation to Social Construction</u>. Thousand Oaks, CA, London: Sage. (Provides a more extended introduction to social constructionist ideas and their implications for research and practice.)

Gergen, Mary & Davis, Sara N. (Eds.) (1997). <u>Toward a New Psychology of Gender</u>. New York: Routledge. (Includes discussions of social constructionism and its relationship to feminist thought.)

Gergen, Mary & Gergen, Kenneth J., (Eds.) (2003). <u>Social Construction: A Reader</u>. London: Sage. (A collection of classic and contemporary contributions to social constructionist theory and practice.)

Potter, Jonathan (1996). <u>Representing Reality</u>. London: Sage. (This sophisticated work places special emphasis on the use of discourse in constructing human understanding.

Sarbin, Theodore & Kitsuse, John (Eds.) (1994). <u>Constructing the Social</u>. London: Sage. (A collection of engaging contributions to the social construction of our common worlds.)

<u>Positive Aging Newsletter</u>, edited by Ken and Mary Gergen. You may take a look at <u>www.positiveaging.net</u> and even subscribe.

Chapter 2: From Critique to Reconstruction

Bellah, Robert, et al. (1985) <u>Habits of the Heart.</u> Berkeley: University of California press. (A powerful critique of the effects of individualist ideology on personal relationships.)

Frank, Arthur, (1995). The Wounded Storyteller. Chicago: University of Chicago Press.

Gergen, Kenneth J. (1994). Realities and Relationships: Soundings in Social Construction. Cambridge: Harvard University Press. (See especially Chapters 8 & 9 for more on the relational mind.)

Lutz, Catherine (1998). Unnatural Emotions. Chicago: University of Chicago Press. (An excellent account of emotions as constructed by a remote culture.)

Martin, Emily (1987). The Woman in the Body: A Cultural Analysis of Reproduction. Boston: Beacon Press. (Medical anthropologist detailing how social and medical practices create the woman.)

Sampson, Edward E. (1993) Celebrating the Other. Boulder: Westview (An excellent introduction to the shift from self to relationship.)

Chapter 3: Social Construction and Professional Practices

In Therapy:

Anderson, Harlene (1997). Conversation, Language, and Possibilities. New York: Basic Books. (Describes the "not knowing" position in therapy.)

Bohan, Janis and Russell, Glenda (1999). Conversations about Psychology and Sexual Orientation. New York: New York University Press. (Discusses therapy and sexual orientation from a constructionist perspective, while challenging the biological explanation of sexual preferences.)

De Shazer, Steve (1994). Words were Originally Magic. New York: Norton.

McLeod, John (1997). Narrative and Psychotherapy. London: Sage. (An excellent overview of developments in narrative therapy.)

McNamee, Sheila, & Gergen, Kenneth J. (Eds.) (1993). Therapy as Social Construction. London, Thousand Oaks, CA: Sage. (Classic collection of therapists writing about their practices within the social constructionist framework.)

O'Hanlon, William. and Wiener-Davis, M.. (1988). In Search of Solutions: A New Direction in Psychotherapy. New York: Norton. (An early contribution to therapy as reconstruction.)

White, Michael and Epston, David (1990). Narrative Means to Therapeutic Ends. New York: Norton. (A pivotal work in the development of narrative therapy).

In Organizational Development:

Anderson, Harlene, et al. (2001). The Appreciative Organization. Chagrin Falls, OH: Taos Institute Publications. (A brief focus book from the Taos Institute written by the founders who apply appreciative ideas to organizational life.)

Cooperrider, David, & Avital, Michael (Eds.). (2004). Advances in Appreciative Inquiry: Constructive Discourse and Human Organization. New York: Elsevier Publishing. (A collection of articles on AI written by a variety of authors who have studied and practice AI.)

Cooperrider, David, Whitney, Diana, Stavros, Jacqueline. (2003). The Appreciative Inquiry Handbook: For Leaders of Change. Cleveland, Ohio, Lakeshore Publishers.

Cooperrider, David, Sorensen, Peter, J., Whitney, Diana, and Yeager, Therese (Eds). (2000). Appreciative Inquiry: Rethinking Human Organizing Toward a Positive Theory of Change. Stipes Publishing, Champagne, IL.

Drath, Wilfred (2001). The Deep Blue Sea: Rethinking the Source of Leadership. San Francisco: Jossey Bass.

Fry, Ron and Barrett, Frank, et al (Eds.). Appreciative Inquiry: Applications in the Field. Westpoint, CT: Quorum Books. (Case studies relating AI to actual practices).

Schiller, Marge, Holland, Bea Mah, and Riley, Deanna (2001). Appreciative Leaders, Chagrin Falls, OH: Taos Institute Publications. (Interviews and commentary concerning over 20 leaders who were selected for their appreciative approaches to their work.)

Watkins, Jane, and Mohr, Bernard (2001). Appreciative Inquiry: Change at the Speed of Imagination. San Francisco, CA: Jossey-Bass Pfeiffer. (Overview of Appreciative Inquiry by two of its important practitioners.)

Whitney, Diana and Trosten-Bloom, Amanda (2003). The Power of Appreciative Inquiry: A Practical Guide to Positive Change. San Francisco: Berrett-Koehler. (Helpful guide to doing Appreciative Inquiry by two major figures in organizational consulting.)

Whitney, Diana, Cooperrider, David, Trosten-Bloom, Amanda, and Kaplin, Brian (2002) Encylopedia of Positive Questions, Volume one: Using AI to Bring Out the Best in Your Organization. Cleveland, Ohio: Lakeshore Communications. (A useful compendium of AI questions.)

For contemporary developments in Appreciative Inquiry: http://appreciativeinquiry.cwru.edu, a website sponsored by Case Western Reserve University.

The **Taos Institute** offers many workshops in Appreciative Inquiry each year: see www.taosinstitute.net for a full schedule and descriptions.

In Education:

Barbules, N.C. (1993). Dialogue in Teaching. New York: Teacher's College Press. (Using dialogue to enhance teaching practices.)

Bruffee, Kenneth A. (!993). Collaborative Learning, Higher Education, Interdependence, and the Authority of Knowledge. Baltimore, MD: Johns Hopkins University Press. (Important text from one of the leaders of collaborative learning.)

Bruner, Jerome (1996). The Culture of Education. Cambridge, MA: Harvard University Press. (Argues for the cultural construction of education.)

Friere, Paulo (1978). Pedagogy of the Oppressed. Harmondsworth, England: Penguin Books. (A groundbreaking work in the domain of critical education.)

Collaborative writing: www.stanford.edu/group/collaborate.

In Conflict Resolution:

Public Conversations Project: See: www.publicconversations.org. (Includes 25 links to like minded conflict resolution organizations.)

Suskind, L, McKearnan, S. and Thomas-Larmer, J. (Eds.) (1999). The Consensus Building Handbook. Thousand Oaks, CA: Sage. (Workbook for people interested in conflict resolution).

Weiner, E. (Ed.) (1998). The Handbook of Interactive Coexistence. New York: Continuum (An excellent resource for theory and practice in conflict resolution.)

Chapter 4: Research as Constructionist Practice

Bodily, Chris (1995). Ageism and the deployments of "age": a constructionist view. In Sarbin, T. and Kitsuse, J. (Eds.). Constructing the Social. London: Sage.

Daiute, Colette and Lightfoot, Cynthia (Eds.) (2004). Narrative Analysis: Studying the Development of Individuals in Society. London, Thousand Oaks, CA: Sage. (Useful research models, including a chapter by Mary Gergen on her development as a narrative researcher.)

Denzin, Norman and Lincoln, Yvonne (Eds.) (2000). Handbook of Qualitative Research. 2nd. ed. Thousand Oaks, CA: Sage. (Outstanding reference source for developments in qualitative research.)

Ellis, Carolyn and Bochner, Arthur P. (1996). Composing ethnography: Alternative Forms of Qualitative Writing. Walnut Creek, CA: AltaMira Press. (An excellent compilation of creative forms of social science writing.)

Foucault, Michel (1980). Power/knowledge. New York: Pantheon. (An overview of some of Foucault's most important thinking on the relationship of discourse to power.)

Gergen, Mary (2001). Feminist Reconstructions in Psychology: Narrative, Gender and Performance. Thousand Oaks, CA: Sage. (Furnishes a description of her feminist research on narrative and gender, along with examples of performance-oriented inquiry.)

Kuhn, Thomas S. (1970). The Structure of Scientific Revolutions. (2nd, rev. ed.) Chicago: University of Chicago Press. (A book that shook the foundations of scientific enterprise, and helped to establish the social construction of scientific knowledge.)

Lykes, M. Brinton (1997). Dialogue with Guatemalan Indian women: Critical perspectives on constructing collaborative research. In Gergen, M. and Davis, S. (Eds.) Toward a New Psychology of Gender. New York: Routledge. (A description of Lykes' work in Central America in a reader dedicated to the social constructionist approach in feminist psychology.)

Reason, Peter and Bradford, Hilary (2001). Handbook of Action Research. London: Sage. (An excellent compilation of contributions on contemporary action research.)

Ronai, Carol Rambo (2002.) The next night sous rature: Wrestling with Derrida's mimesis. In N. K. Denzin & Y S. Lincoln (Eds.). The Qualitative Inquiry Reader (pp. 105-124). London, Thousand Oaks, CA: Sage. (Example of autoethnography by a "pole dancer" in a highly recommended resource for alternative qualitative methods.)

Chapter 5: From Critique to Collaboration

Gergen, Kenneth J. (1994). Realities and Relationships. Cambridge: Harvard University Press. (Offers extended discussion on critiques from the camps of both the empirical and the ideologically committed standpoints.)

Hacking, Ian (1999). The Social Construction of What? Cambridge: Harvard University Press. (A philosopher works through the problems created for scientific knowledge by constructionist thought.)

Hepburn, Alexa (2003). Relativism and feminist psychology, In M. Gergen & K. Gergen (Eds.) Social Construction: A Reader. (pp. 237-247). London, Thousand Oaks, CA: Sage. (An excellent rebuttal to charges of relativism made to feminist social constructionist positions.)

Hermans, C.A.M., Immink, G., de Jong, A., and van der Lans, J. (Eds.) (2002). Social Constructionism and Theology. Leiden: Brill. (Attempts to extend constructionist thought to issues of theology and religious practice.)

Parker, Ian (1998). Social Constructionism, Discourse and Realism. London: Sage. (Offers critical deliberation on relationships between realist and constructionist orientations.)

Smith, Barbara (1997). <u>Belief and Resistance</u>. Cambridge: Harvard University Press. (A sophisticated defense against essentialist and realist critiques.)

More resources from Kenneth and Mary Gergen can be found on their websites:

Kenneth Gergen- http://www.swarthmore.edu/SocSci/kgergen1

Mary Gergen- http://www.de.psu.edu/Faculty/gergen/gergen.html